OPPOSING
VIEWPOINTS®
SERIES

Natural Gas

Other Books of Related Interest:

Opposing Viewpoints Series
Renewable Energy

At Issue Series
Fracking

Hybrid and Electric Cars

Current Controversies Series
Gasoline

"Congress shall make
no law . . . abridging
the freedom of speech,
or of the press."

First Amendment to the US Constitution

The basic foundation of our democracy is the First Amendment guarantee of freedom of expression. The Opposing Viewpoints series is dedicated to the concept of this basic freedom and the idea that it is more important to practice it than to enshrine it.

OPPOSING
VIEWPOINTS®
SERIES

I Natural Gas

Dedria Bryfonski, Book Editor

GREENHAVEN PRESS
A part of Gale, Cengage Learning

GALE
CENGAGE Learning·

Farmington Hills, Mich • San Francisco • New York • Waterville, Maine
Meriden, Conn • Mason, Ohio • Chicago

Patricia Coryell, *Vice President & Publisher, New Products & GVRL*
Douglas Dentino, *Manager, New Products*
Judy Galens, *Acquisitions Editor*

© 2015 Greenhaven Press, a part of Gale, Cengage Learning.

WCN: 01-100-101

For more information, contact:
Greenhaven Press
27500 Drake Rd.
Farmington Hills, MI 48331-3535
Or you can visit our Internet site at http://www.gale.cengage.com

For product information and technology assistance, contact us at

Gale Customer Support, 1-800-877-4253
For permission to use material from this text or product, submit all requests online at www.cengage.com/permissions

Further permissions questions can be emailed to permissionrequest@cengage.com

Articles in Greenhaven Press anthologies are often edited for length to meet page requirements. In addition, original titles of these works are changed to clearly present the main thesis and to explicitly indicate the author's opinion. Every effort is made to ensure that Greenhaven Press accurately reflects the original intent of the authors. Every effort has been made to trace the owners of copyrighted material.

Cover Image © Pakhnyushcha/Shutterstock.com.

LIBRARY OF CONGRESS CATALOGING-IN-PUBLICATION DATA

Natural gas / Dedria Bryfonski, book editor.
    pages cm. -- (Opposing viewpoints)
    Includes bibliographical references and index.
    ISBN 978-0-7377-7276-0 (hardcover) -- ISBN 978-0-7377-7277-7 (pbk.)
    1. Hydraulic fracturing--Environmental aspects. 2. Natural gas--Prospecting--Environmental aspects. 3. Natural gas--Geology. I. Bryfonski, Dedria, editor.
    TN278.N38 2015
    333.8'2330973--dc23
                                                      2014025084

Printed in the United States of America
1 2 3 4 5 6 7 18 17 16 15 14

Contents

Chapter 3: Should the United States Export Natural Gas?

Chapter 4: Should Offshore Drilling for Gas Be Permitted?

Why Consider Opposing Viewpoints?

> *"The only way in which a human being can make some approach to knowing the whole of a subject is by hearing what can be said about it by persons of every variety of opinion and studying all modes in which it can be looked at by every character of mind. No wise man ever acquired his wisdom in any mode but this."*
>
> John Stuart Mill

In our media-intensive culture it is not difficult to find differing opinions. Thousands of newspapers and magazines and dozens of radio and television talk shows resound with differing points of view. The difficulty lies in deciding which opinion to agree with and which "experts" seem the most credible. The more inundated we become with differing opinions and claims, the more essential it is to hone critical reading and thinking skills to evaluate these ideas. Opposing Viewpoints books address this problem directly by presenting stimulating debates that can be used to enhance and teach these skills. The varied opinions contained in each book examine many different aspects of a single issue. While examining these conveniently edited opposing views, readers can develop critical thinking skills such as the ability to compare and contrast authors' credibility, facts, argumentation styles, use of persuasive techniques, and other stylistic tools. In short, the Opposing Viewpoints Series is an ideal way to attain the higher-level thinking and reading skills so essential in a culture of diverse and contradictory opinions.

In addition to providing a tool for critical thinking, Opposing Viewpoints books challenge readers to question their own strongly held opinions and assumptions. Most people form their opinions on the basis of upbringing, peer pressure, and personal, cultural, or professional bias. By reading carefully balanced opposing views, readers must directly confront new ideas as well as the opinions of those with whom they disagree. This is not to argue simplistically that everyone who reads opposing views will—or should—change his or her opinion. Instead, the series enhances readers' understanding of their own views by encouraging confrontation with opposing ideas. Careful examination of others' views can lead to the readers' understanding of the logical inconsistencies in their own opinions, perspective on why they hold an opinion, and the consideration of the possibility that their opinion requires further evaluation.

Evaluating Other Opinions

To ensure that this type of examination occurs, Opposing Viewpoints books present all types of opinions. Prominent spokespeople on different sides of each issue as well as well-known professionals from many disciplines challenge the reader. An additional goal of the series is to provide a forum for other, less known, or even unpopular viewpoints. The opinion of an ordinary person who has had to make the decision to cut off life support from a terminally ill relative, for example, may be just as valuable and provide just as much insight as a medical ethicist's professional opinion. The editors have two additional purposes in including these less known views. One, the editors encourage readers to respect others' opinions—even when not enhanced by professional credibility. It is only by reading or listening to and objectively evaluating others' ideas that one can determine whether they are worthy of consideration. Two, the inclusion of such viewpoints encourages the important critical thinking skill of objectively evaluating an author's credentials and bias. This evaluation will illuminate an author's reasons for taking a particular stance on an issue and will aid in readers' evaluation of the author's ideas.

It is our hope that these books will give readers a deeper understanding of the issues debated and an appreciation of the complexity of even seemingly simple issues when good and honest people disagree. This awareness is particularly important in a democratic society such as ours in which people enter into public debate to determine the common good. Those with whom one disagrees should not be regarded as enemies but rather as people whose views deserve careful examination and may shed light on one's own.

Thomas Jefferson once said that "difference of opinion leads to inquiry, and inquiry to truth." Jefferson, a broadly educated man, argued that "if a nation expects to be ignorant and free . . . it expects what never was and never will be." As individuals and as a nation, it is imperative that we consider the opinions of others and examine them with skill and discernment. The Opposing Viewpoints series is intended to help readers achieve this goal.

David L. Bender and Bruno Leone,
Founders

Introduction

"The energy outlook for natural gas has changed dramatically over the past several years. The most significant story is the transformative role played by shale gas."

—Richard G. Newell,
former head of the US Energy
Information Administration
and professor at Duke University

Natural gas is a fossil fuel that most scientists believe was created in prehistoric time as billions of plants and animals absorbed energy from the sun—energy that was stored as carbon molecules in their bodies. When these organisms died, they drifted to the bottoms of oceans. These layers, covered by sand and mud, piled up over millions of years. As the layers became thicker and formed into rock, their weight produced pressure and heat that changed the decaying matter into oil and gas. The primary component of natural gas is methane with smaller amounts of hydrocarbons such as ethane, butane, and propane. Impurities such as water, carbon dioxide, and hydrogen sulfide are also found in some fields of natural gas.

The first discovery of natural gas is generally believed to have occurred in southeastern Asia sometime between 6000 and 2000 B.C., as natural gas began seeping up in the Baku region of what is now Azerbaijan. Some seeps were ignited—most likely by lightning—and were believed by the ancient Persians to have supernatural powers. According to "History of Chinese Invention—The Discovery of Natural Gas," at Computersmiths.com,

One of the most famous of these types of flames was found in ancient Greece, on Mount Parnassus approximately 1000 B.C. A goat herdsman came across what looked like a "burning spring," a flame rising from a fissure in the rock. The Greeks, believing it to be of divine origin, built a temple on the flame. This temple housed a priestess who was known as the Oracle of Delphi, giving out prophecies she claimed were inspired by the flame.

The ancient Chinese were the first to find a practical use for natural gas, according to most scientists. In approximately 500 B.C., the Chinese discovered pockets of flammable gas in areas where they were drilling for brine. Using bamboo tubes, the Chinese extracted both brine and gas and used the gas to heat the brine to create drinking water. By about the second century B.C., the Chinese began routing gas from one area to another in pipelines constructed from bamboo.

It would be many more centuries before commercial uses were found for natural gas. According to the American Public Gas Association, the first commercialized use of natural gas was in England, where beginning about 1785 the natural gas produced from coal was used to light houses and streets. In 1816, Baltimore became the first American city to use gas streetlights. The modern history of natural gas was initiated in 1821 when William Hart dug a twenty-seven-foot gas well in Fredonia, New York. The Fredonia Gas Light Company was formed and was the first natural gas distribution company in the United States. Throughout most of the 1800s, gas was used primarily for streetlights, as there were no pipelines to bring gas directly into homes.

Another watershed moment in the history of natural gas occurred in 1885 when Robert Bunsen invented what is now called the Bunsen burner, a device that mixed natural gas with air to produce a flame. This invention created new ways to use gas for cooking and heating.

The first lengthy pipeline was built in 1891 and connected central Indiana to Chicago. In the early 1900s, large fields of natural gas were discovered in Texas and Oklahoma.

It wasn't until after World War II, however, that a pipeline network was built that would facilitate the widespread use of natural gas. Concerned during the war that German submarines were targeting oil tankers, the US government authorized the construction of an oil pipeline from Texas to the East Coast. Following the war, this pipeline was used for transporting gas as well as oil. Using a modern seamless steel pipe introduced in the 1920s, gas could be transported under higher pressure and in greater quantities. By 1950, almost three hundred thousand miles of gas pipeline had been laid. Once it became economical to transport natural gas, its uses expanded. Gas is now used in appliances such as water heaters, ovens, furnaces, stoves, and clothes dryers. Natural gas also supplies energy for manufacturing and processing. The use of natural gas grew steadily throughout the mid-twentieth century. As political events in the Middle East threatened the worldwide supply of oil, natural gas became an even more important source of energy. In 2014, natural gas represented approximately 25 percent of all energy used in the United States.

While natural gas is expected to remain an important energy source in the future, several controversies surround its production and use. In the viewpoints that follow, scientists, commentators, and journalists offer varying opinions on the issues surrounding natural gas in chapters that ask "Should Fracking Be Permitted?," "Does the United States Need More Gas Pipeline Capacity?," "Should the United States Export Natural Gas?," and "Should Offshore Drilling for Gas Be Permitted?" The provocative viewpoints in *Opposing Viewpoints: Natural Gas* give the reader an idea of the complexity and difficulty of the issues surrounding natural gas in the new millennium.

OPPOSING
VIEWPOINTS®
SERIES

CHAPTER 1

Should Fracking Be Permitted?

Chapter Preface

In 2008, concern about dwindling supplies of natural gas drove prices to $15 per million cubic feet. Just three years later, the International Energy Agency was predicting that the world had sufficient supplies of natural gas to last 250 years, and gas prices plummeted to $4 per million cubic feet. According to James Mulva, chief executive of ConocoPhillips, speaking at the World Petroleum Congress in December 2011, "The world holds centuries of natural gas supply, enough for generations. We don't need any new miracles, the miracles have already occurred." Foremost among the miracles Mulva was citing was the technology of hydraulic fracturing, commonly known as fracking.

For decades, gas was extracted from hydrocarbons that had seeped out of layers of sedimentary rock and collected into large pools relatively near the surface. Drilling for natural gas was a relatively simply technology to master, as the natural pressure of the earth would send gas to the surface when the pools were drilled into. However, there were only a limited number of known pools, which led to a concern that the earth's gas reservoirs would someday be depleted.

George Mitchell, a Texas oil man, had a different idea—to drill deeper, directly to the sedimentary rock holding the oil and gas—and he doggedly pursued this concept for almost twenty years before succeeding. The Mitchell Energy and Development Corporation hit pay dirt in 1998 by drilling straight down, making a ninety-degree turn to penetrate shale formations horizontally, and then injecting a high-pressure mix of water, sand, and chemicals to crack open the rock and release the gas. Following Mitchell's death in July 2013, energy historian Daniel Yergin stated,

> "He is responsible for what is the most important innovation in world energy so far this century. Before his break-

through, shale gas had another name—'uneconomic' gas. It was thought that there was no way to commercially extract it. He proved that it could be done. His breakthrough in hydraulic fracturing, when combined with horizontal drilling, set off the revolution in unconventional oil and gas that we see today. But it did not come easily. It took a decade and a half of conviction, investment and dogged determination. In the face of great skepticism and refusing to accept 'no' as an answer, Mitchell dramatically changed America's energy position. As such, he also changed the world energy outlook in the 21st century and set in motion the global rebalancing of oil and gas that is now occurring."

Although scientists are in agreement that fracking has changed the worldwide energy landscape, there is less agreement on the impact that this technology has on the environment. In the chapter that follows, scientists, commentators, and journalists debate the environmental, safety, and economic issues surrounding fracking.

| "The shale-gas boom will provide a
modest boost to U.S. economic growth."

The Shale-Gas Boom Won't Do Much for Climate Change. But It Will Make Us Richer

Brad Plumer

Brad Plumer is a reporter who covers energy and environmental issues for the Washington Post. *In the following viewpoint, he reports that a 2013 study by Stanford University's Energy Modeling Forum shows that the natural gas boom will provide a modest boost of approximately $70 billion each year to the US gross domestic product. While natural gas is cleaner than coal, it is not as clean as nuclear, wind, and solar energy, he explains. Because natural gas is so cheap and plentiful, there will be less incentive to turn to these cleaner sources, Plumer surmises, and thus there will be a negligible impact on climate change.*

As you read, consider the following questions:

1. According to Plumer, why is the economic impact of the shale-gas boom so modest?

2. What impact will the increased use of natural gas have on air pollutants other than carbon dioxide?

3. According to the viewpoint, why is there such a great disparity in natural gas price forecasts?

The shale-gas boom in the United States won't, by itself, keep driving down U.S. carbon-dioxide emissions in the years ahead. That's because, in addition to killing off coal-fired plants, cheap gas will also crowd out cleaner energy sources like wind, solar, and nuclear.

The Shale-Gas Boom Benefits the Economy

On the other hand, the glut of natural gas from fracking will make the country a bit wealthier and clean up other harmful air pollutants from power plants.

Those are the conclusions of a big new report ["Changing the Game?: Emissions and Market Implications of New Natural Gas Supplies," September 2013] from Stanford's Energy Modeling Forum, which convened 50 experts and 14 different modeling teams from industry, academia, and government to look at how the surge in natural-gas production could transform the U.S. economy.

Here are four key points:

1) *The shale-gas boom will provide a modest boost to U.S. economic growth.* On average, the models in the Stanford study predicted that the natural-gas boom would raise GDP [gross domestic product] by about $70 billion each year over the next several decades (in current dollars). "Although this amount appears large," the report notes, "it represents a relatively modest 0.46 percent of the U.S. economy."

Why so modest? The surge in natural gas is great for the oil and gas industry, and it will certainly help petrochemical firms that use natural gas as a raw material. Yet these industries are just one slice of the broader U.S. economy, accounting for less than 1 percent of employment. And, while cheaper energy costs do benefit consumers, the impact on GDP is relatively small, all told.

Note that separate consultancy studies . . . have found similar GDP effects but even higher savings for consumers. . . . A lot depends on what the price of gas will do. . . .

2) *The shale-gas boom won't do much to solve climate change—at least not on its own.* In recent years, a glut of natural gas has helped displace coal power in the U.S. power sector and reduce carbon-dioxide emissions significantly. After all, burning natural gas for electricity produces about half the carbon dioxide that burning coal does.

Yet many of the experts in the Stanford study don't expect carbon emissions to keep falling—at least not without further policy changes. That's because cheap natural gas is also likely to displace even cleaner sources of energy like nuclear, wind, and solar. What's more, low natural-gas prices will discourage efforts to conserve energy and boost efficiency.

As a result, most models expect U.S. carbon emissions to rise between 2010 and 2035, whether shale-gas production is low . . . or high. . . .

A few models do expect overall carbon-dioxide emissions to drop in the coming decades purely as a result of the shale-gas boom. . . . But those models are in the minority, and even they predict a modest drop. Bigger cuts in emissions would likely require Congress to place a price on carbon. . . .

Most experts in the Stanford study expect natural gas to displace coal, nuclear, and renewable energy between now and 2035: The upshot here is that fracking won't solve climate change on its own. . . .

3) *Natural gas will, however, help clean up other air pollutants.* There's some good environmental news here. Natural gas is considerably cleaner than coal when it comes to other types of harmful air pollution, such as sulfur dioxide and nitrogen dioxide. These pollutants are expected to drop as shale gas becomes more plentiful.

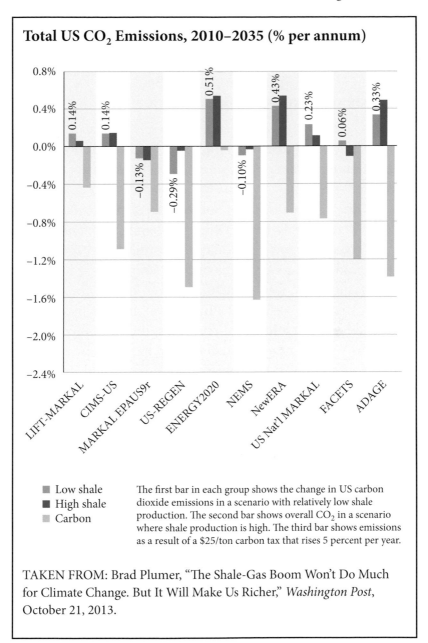

Total US CO$_2$ Emissions, 2010–2035 (% per annum)

Low shale
High shale
Carbon

The first bar in each group shows the change in US carbon dioxide emissions in a scenario with relatively low shale production. The second bar shows overall CO$_2$ in a scenario where shale production is high. The third bar shows emissions as a result of a $25/ton carbon tax that rises 5 percent per year.

TAKEN FROM: Brad Plumer, "The Shale-Gas Boom Won't Do Much for Climate Change. But It Will Make Us Richer," *Washington Post*, October 21, 2013.

Cleaner air, in turn, will make the country slightly richer by improving health and extending lives, "average emission damages decline by $1 billion each year (2010 dollars) for sulfur dioxide and by $0.25 billion each year for nitrogen oxides," the study notes.

Forecasts on Economic Benefits Vary

4) *There's a fair bit of disagreement between forecasts.* Note that we've mainly been discussing the aggregate conclusions of all these different models. But some of the forecasts do vary significantly.

One key variable is price: Some experts expect natural-gas prices to stay roughly flat between now and 2020, going from $4 per thousand cubic feet today to around $4.03 by the end of the decade. Others expect a sharper jump upward to $6.23 per thousand cubic feet by 2020 and even higher thereafter.

Why so much variation? "Important factors include the costs of developing additional resources, the flexibility by consumers in seeking new applications for natural gas, and policies that affect fuel choice by electric utilities and end users. Particularly important are regulations that facilitate more or less expansion in nuclear, solar, wind or energy-efficiency opportunities."

The price assumptions can make a big difference here. For instance, the study notes that every $1 drop in the price of a thousand cubic feet of natural gas can boost the economy by around $55 billion.

"Fracking has sent the price of natural gas plummeting, just not for the people who need it most."

Consumers See Little Economic Benefit from Fracking

Patrick Reis

Patrick Reis is policy editor for National Journal. *He previously worked at* Politico, Greenwire, *and Seattle's* Real Change. *In the following viewpoint, Reis reports that the price of natural gas bought directly from drillers has dropped two-thirds between 2008 and 2012. This price break is not passed along proportionally to consumers, whose household budgets are tight, he continues. The gap is due to infrastructure costs, as gas utility companies need to invest in additional pipelines, and they pass these costs on to the consumer, Reis concludes.*

As you read, consider the following questions:

1. According to Reis, what was the cost of natural gas for direct buyers in 2008 and in 2012?

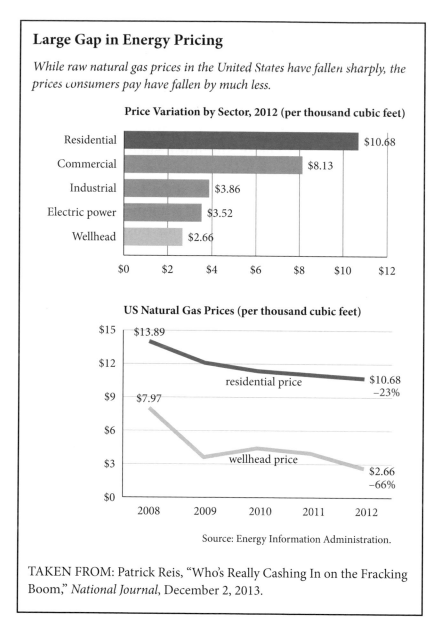

Large Gap in Energy Pricing

While raw natural gas prices in the United States have fallen sharply, the prices consumers pay have fallen by much less.

Price Variation by Sector, 2012 (per thousand cubic feet)

Residential $10.68
Commercial $8.13
Industrial $3.86
Electric power $3.52
Wellhead $2.66

$0 $2 $4 $6 $8 $10 $12

US Natural Gas Prices (per thousand cubic feet)

$15 $13.89
$12
residential price $10.68
$9 $7.97 −23%
$6
$3 wellhead price $2.66
$0 −66%

2008 2009 2010 2011 2012

Source: Energy Information Administration.

TAKEN FROM: Patrick Reis, "Who's Really Cashing In on the Fracking Boom," *National Journal*, December 2, 2013.

Instead, utility rates vary based on how much a company spends on connecting customers with the gas supplies, and that's where consumers may see new costs. As gas has gotten cheaper, more customers are looking to get it delivered to their homes and businesses, and that has driven demand for utilities to expand the pipelines and other amenities they use to deliver gas to homes.

And unlike raw material costs, those infrastructure costs do get passed from utilities to consumers in the form of higher gas bills.

"To some extent, what a consumer pays is going to follow, at a lag, the energy markets," Sweeney said. "But other things—a hookup charge, a delivery charge, taxes—those can be a pretty strong component of what a customer pays."

> *"Fracking is a 'safe and effective' tech-*
> *nology for producing energy from deep*
> *geological formations."*

Fracking Is Safe

Rock Zierman

Rock Zierman is chief executive officer of the California Inde-
pendent Petroleum Association. In the following viewpoint, he
asserts that numerous studies have concluded that fracking is a
safe technology that poses no threat to air or water quality and
does not cause earthquakes. Despite these studies and the sup-
port for fracking by agencies such as the US Environmental Pro-
tection Agency, the US Department of Energy, and the Ground-
water Protection Council, anti-fracking activists make
exaggerated claims of problems associated with the process, Zier-
man maintains. He says that regulation of fracking is necessary
and that there should be an ongoing effort to ensure that the
public is well informed but that banning fracking makes no eco-
nomic or environmental sense.

As you read, consider the following questions:

1. What were the conclusions of a 2009 study from the US
   Department of Energy and the Groundwater Protection
   Council, according to the viewpoint?

2. What evidence does the author cite to dismiss activists' claims that fracking results in excessive demands on the water supply?

3. What evidence does the author cite to dismiss activists' claims that fracking contributes to earthquakes?

Hydraulic fracturing has been routinely used for more than 60 years to produce oil and natural gas. But is it safe?

This question has been asked and answered many times over by government regulators, scientists, and other technical experts, and they have all concluded that hydraulic fracturing is a fundamentally safe technology. Interior secretaries, energy secretaries and Environmental Protection Agency (EPA) heads have repeatedly said that fracking can be done, and is being done, so that it doesn't present environmental or public health problems.

That's been the case for decades, said [President Barack] Obama's interior secretary Sally Jewell last May [2013]. Jewell's predecessor, Ken Salazar, testified to Congress that hydraulic fracturing "has been done safely hundreds of thousands of times" and warned lawmakers against anti-fracking "hysteria."

Fracking Does Not Contaminate Water

As far back as 1995, the EPA studied whether hydraulic fracturing contaminated drinking water. The EPA studied a site in Alabama at the request of environmentalists and found "no evidence" of "any contamination or endangerment of underground sources of drinking water." In 2004, the agency conducted a broader study and also found fracking "poses little or no threat" to water supplies.

In 2009, another study from the U.S. Department of Energy and the Groundwater Protection Council—an interstate body of environmental regulators—concluded that fracking is a "safe and effective" technology for producing energy from deep geological formations.

More recently, Stanford University geophysicist Mark Zoback, who's also served as an advisor to the Obama administration, confirmed fluids used in hydraulic fracturing "have not contaminated any water supply," and with more than a mile of impermeable rock separating deep shale and shallow drinking water aquifers, "it is very unlikely they could." In California, it is worth noting, more than 90% of hydraulic fracturing occurs in parts of Kern County where there is no potable groundwater.

Anti-Oil and Gas Activists Exaggerate Concerns

Anti–domestic oil and gas forces respond to such good news by finding new ways to scare the public. That's why you hear more and more allegations about air quality and water use. On air quality, they are ignoring that California's oil and gas industry has operated under some of the world's tightest emission controls which have cut fugitive emissions even while drilling activity has risen.

Next, activists exaggerate problems associated with water usage and produced water disposal associated with hydraulic fracturing. In states where hydraulic fracturing is used much more frequently, and where many times as much water is used as in California, the process accounts for less than 1% of total water demand according to the Department of Energy and the Groundwater Protection Council. In addition, wastewater can be treated and reused, minimizing both issues.

In California, we use much less water than other states because of our geology. For perspective, the amount of water used in all of the hydraulic fracturing jobs in California last year was about the same as the amount of water the state's golf courses consumed in half a day.

US Department of the Interior Says Fracking Is Safe

"As the president [Barack Obama] has made clear, this administration's priority is to continue to expand safe and responsible domestic energy production. In line with that goal, we are proposing some commonsense updates that increase safety while also providing flexibility and facilitating coordination with states and tribes," said Secretary of the Interior Sally Jewell. "As we continue to offer millions of acres of America's public lands for oil and gas development, it is important that the public has full confidence that the right safety and environmental protections are in place.". . .

"We know from experience that hydraulic fracturing and horizontal drilling methods can be used safely and effectively, employing many of the best management practices reflected in this draft rule," said BLM [Bureau of Land Management] principal deputy director Neil Kornze. "Our thorough review of all the comments convinced us that we could maintain a strong level of protection of health, safety, and the environment while allowing for increased flexibility and reduced regulatory duplication."

"Interior Releases Updated Draft Rule for Hydraulic Fracturing on Public and Indian Lands for Public Comment,"
Bureau of Land Management,
US Department of the Interior, May 16, 2013.

As for earthquakes, a yearlong study released in 2012, the first of its kind in the state, at the Inglewood Oil Field in the Baldwin Hills area found "no detectable effects on vibration"— and no water- or air-quality problems either—from hydraulic fracturing. Perhaps that's because, as Zoback has explained, the amount of seismic energy released during hydraulic fracturing is about the same as "a gallon of milk falling off the kitchen counter." In fact, the National Research Council concluded last year that hydraulic fracturing does not pose a high risk of inducing earthquakes. The separate process of injecting oil- and gas-produced water into deep disposal wells has never triggered an earthquake in California despite tens of thousands of active injection wells that have operated for decades.

Happily, there is a bipartisan political consensus in California to go along with the scientific consensus that responsible and regulated hydraulic fracturing is safe and is a great benefit to our state. Governor [Jerry] Brown, one of the nation's leading environmental advocates, was very clear that he and the regulators at the Division of Oil, Gas and Geothermal Resources (DOGGR) would let science be their guide, rather than, as he put it, "jumping on any ideological bandwagons."

Following DOGGR's lead, the governor and the large majority of the heavily Democratic legislature opposed several fracking moratorium bills and instead passed SB 4, California's new comprehensive regulations on well stimulation. Under SB 4, the industry now operates under even more strict regulation than before, with a host of fracking-specific rules designed to make the process even more transparent and to address the concerns that many Californians have expressed in the wake of the activist misinformation campaign.

Producers now have to pre-notify both regulators as well as surrounding residents and property owners before doing any hydraulic fracturing. They must post on a public website all chemicals used in the process as well as amounts of water and disposal methods. They must obtain an approved groundwater monitoring program that ensures no fluids are escaping the wellbore.

Hydraulic fracturing has dramatically lowered greenhouse gas emissions in the United States because fracking is required for natural gas development in other areas of the country. President Obama—certainly a strong environmentalist—acknowledged this when he said, "We should strengthen our position as the top natural gas producer because in the medium term at least it not only can provide safe, cheap power, but it can also help reduce our carbon emissions."

Regulators should continue to review the rules that apply for hydraulic fracturing and find ways to improve them to ensure that the public has the information it needs about the process. The facts clearly show that this technology can be used safely as has been the case for the last 60 years.

| *"60 percent of oil and gas wells failed within 28 years."*

Fracking Is Not Safe

Anthony Ingraffea

Anthony Ingraffea is the Dwight C. Baum professor of engineering at Cornell University. In the following viewpoint, he contends that despite claims to the contrary by those in the gas and oil industry, problems that arise during the fracking process can release toxins into the air and water. Most of the problems that occur can be traced to the difficulty of getting the cement job right, he explains. Ingraffea suggests that to preserve water and air quality and reduce carbon emissions, America should turn to renewable wind, water, and solar energy technologies, not fracking.

As you read, consider the following questions:

1. What is the failure rate of oil and gas wells, according to the author?

2. According to the viewpoint, what are some of the environmental factors that can lead to cement damage?

3. According to Ingraffea, what leakage rates were found by the National Oceanic and Atmospheric Administration at gas and oil fields in California, Colorado, and Utah?

Many people have embraced hydraulic fracturing's new wave of oil and gas development in shale as a 'bridge' to a clean energy future. As a longtime oil and gas engineer who helped develop shale fracking techniques for the Energy Department, I know these technological advancements have not equated to making oil and gas development a cleaner extractive industry.

Cement Failures Are Common

Fracking is an extreme form of fossil fuel development because of the large number of big wells that have to be drilled to develop these deep oil and gas resources. Unconventional oil and gas drilling requires directional drilling, high frack fluid volume, slickwater (fracking fluid water that has been laced with a lubricant because contrary to what you'd think, water isn't slippery or viscous enough to do the job), multiwell pads and cluster drilling. These technologies put drinking water at risk for contamination with biocides, heavy metals, salts, radioactive materials, endocrine disruptors and oils.

While operators repeatedly claim that their technology is safe, those of us who understand the industry can tell you that problems frequently occur. It is often said within the industry that the three biggest problems are cement, cement, and cement. It is difficult to do a perfect cement job. The BP oil well failure in the Gulf of Mexico [in 2010] was a result of a shoddy cementing job. The cement has to bond to a grease-coated steel pipe on one side and with the rocks, minerals, and mud on the other side. The problem is if the outside layer of cement fails, the inside layer doesn't matter. According to a review of industry's own data, 60 percent of oil and gas wells

Fracking Challenges the Water Supply

Development and production of oil and gas resources can also require and yield significant quantities of water. Produced water and fluids used and recovered during hydrofracturing (hydrofracking) are likely to play an expanding role in energy resource considerations because treatment and disposal costs for produced and hydrofracking waters vary markedly. Also, the potential beneficial use of produced waters is an area of expanding interest, particularly in areas with limited water resources.

"Hydraulic Fracturing," US Geological Survey, US Department of the Interior, December 19, 2013.

failed within 28 years. These failures can lead to the contamination of the aquifers we need to keep clean for drinking water.

Multiple industry studies show that about 5 percent of all oil and gas wells leak immediately because of integrity issues, with increasing rates of leakage over time. With hundreds of thousands of new wells expected, this problem is neither negligible nor preventable with current technology.

Pressures under the earth, temperature changes, ground movement from the drilling of nearby wells, and shrinkage crack and damage the thin layer of brittle cement that is supposed to seal the wells. And remember, getting the cement perfect as the drilling goes horizontally into shale or other tight formations is extremely challenging. Once the cement is damaged, repairing it thousands of feet underground is expensive and often unsuccessful. The oil and gas industry has been trying to solve this problem for decades.

Fracking Risks Contaminating Air and Water

The scientific community has been waiting for better data from the EPA [Environmental Protection Agency] to assess the extent of the water contamination problem. That is why it is so discouraging that, in the face of industry complaints, the EPA reportedly has closed or backed away from several investigations into the problem. Perhaps a full EPA study of hydraulic fracturing and drinking water, due in 2014, will be more forthcoming. In addition, drafts of an Energy Department study suggest that there are huge problems finding enough water for fracturing future wells. Water quantity impacts may be even more severe than water quality impacts.

And risks aren't just to water resources. Another problem is that methane routinely leaks from these unconventional wells. Though there is significant uncertainty over the rate, recent measurements by the National Oceanic and Atmospheric Administration at gas and oil fields in California, Colorado and Utah found leakage rates of 2.3 percent to 17 percent of annual production, in the range my colleagues at Cornell [University] and I predicted some years ago. This is the gas that is released into the atmosphere unburned as part of the hydraulic fracturing process, and also from pipelines, compressors and processing units. Those findings raise questions about what is happening elsewhere. The Environmental Protection Agency has issued new rules to reduce these emissions, but the rules don't take effect until 2015, and apply only to new gas wells.

We have renewable wind, water, solar and energy-efficiency technology options now. We can scale these quickly and affordably, creating economic growth, jobs and a truly clean energy future. Political will is the missing ingredient. Protection of our water and air, as well as meaningful carbon reduction, is impossible so long as the fossil fuel industry is allowed so much influence over our energy policies and regulatory agencies. Policy makers need to listen to the voices of independent scientists while there is still time.

> "We have wasted a lot of time that should have gone into seriously looking into and developing alternative energies."

Fracking Contributes to Global Warming

Louis W. Allstadt, as told to Ellen Cantarow

Louis W. Allstadt is a retired executive vice president of Mobil oil corporation. Ellen Cantarow is a journalist whose work on Israel and Palestine has been widely published for thirty years. In the following viewpoint, Allstadt explains that fracking is far more dangerous than conventional drilling because of the increased possibility that methane gas will be released into the atmosphere. He explains this is because of two factors: Fracking requires fifty to one hundred times more fracking fluids, which produces more flowback than conventional wells, and the rock above the target zone tends to be less impervious, which can cause methane gas to creep up to the surface and into the atmosphere. He concludes that more attention should be paid to developing clean energy sources.

41

Ellen Cantarow: So could you describe the dangers of this in-dustry?

First of all you have to look at what is conventional oil and gas. That was pretty much anything that was produced until around 2000. It's basically a process of drilling down through a cap rock, an impervious rock that has trapped oil and gas beneath it—sometimes only gas. If it's oil, there's always gas with it. And once you're into that reservoir—which is really not a void, it's porous rock—the natural pressure of the gas will push up the gas and oil. Typically you'll have a well that will keep going 20, 30 years before you have to do something to boost the production through a secondary recovery mechanism. That conventional process is basically what was used from the earliest wells in Pennsylvania through most of the offshore production that exists now, that started in the shallow water in the Gulf of Mexico and gradually moved down into deeper and deeper water.

Now what's happened is that the prospect of finding more of those conventional reservoirs, particularly on land and in the places that have been heavily explored like the US and Europe and the Middle East just is very, very small. And the companies have pretty much acknowledged that. All of them talk about the need to go to either nonconventional shale or tight sand drilling or to go into deeper and deeper waters or to go into really hostile Arctic regions and possibly Antarctic regions.

Methane Release: Fracking the Planet's Future

So when you talked about "the race for what's left," that's what's going on. Both the horizontal drilling and fracturing have been around for a long time. The industry will tell you this over and over again—they've been around for 60 years, things like that. That is correct. What's different is the volume of fracking fluids and the volume of flowback that occurs in these wells. It is 50 to 100 times more than what was used in the conventional wells.

The other [difference] is that the rock above the target zone is not necessarily impervious the way it was in the conventional wells. And to me that last point is at least as big as the volume. The industry will tell you that the mile or two between the zone that's being fracked is not going to let anything come up.

But there are already cases where the methane gas has made it up into the aquifers and atmosphere. Sometimes through old well bores, sometimes through natural fissures in the rock. What we don't know is just how much gas is going to come up over time. It's a point most people haven't gotten. It's not just what's happening today. We're opening up channels for the gas to creep up to the surface and into the atmosphere. And methane is a much more potent greenhouse gas in the short term—less than 100 years—than carbon dioxide.

Methane-Migration Evidence and the DEC

Was there any major turning point that started you thinking about methane migration?

There were many. An example is that one of the appendices of the draft SGEIS that was issued in July 2011 had a section describing an EPA [Environmental Protection Agency] study of the only cases where similar fractures had been unearthed. These were in a coal mining area. The EPA investigation indicated that the fractures had progressed in unexpected patterns and at greater lengths than expected. In September, when the draft SGEIS was eventually put out for comment, that section had been expunged.

That's shocking! I know a lot has been discovered about the collusion between New York's DEC and the industry. Is this one big example?

Yes, it is. To ignore the only direct evidence of fractures, or to remove it from public information, indicates that the industry was trying to hide something. The other point is that in terms of a turning point (in my thinking), here is evidence that the fractures go further and in patterns that were not expected. It showed that fractures could allow methane to reach drinking water aquifers or the atmosphere. . . .

A Quiet Retirement Gets Fracked

I retired with no intention of doing anything in the oil or gas industries. [But] about the time we bought this house and started restoration, people that knew I had been in the oil business started saying, what do you think about fracking? I had not been following it at all, and said, 'What do you mean?' They said, 'They're talking about maybe drilling gas wells 100 or 150 feet from the lake.' I said, 'That's crazy. It doesn't make any sense, I'll see what I can find out.'

That's where it started. I started looking into it, realized what the new process was, and looked at the New York State regulations, and at that point they were just starting to draft the first version of the SGEIS, and they were just horrible. They didn't make sense even for conventional drilling, most of them, they were so weak.

Initially I put together a little presentation. People started asking me if I would talk about it. It just happens that there are a few people within a couple miles of here that know something about it. We had different approaches, different styles, but we would share information. The focus at that time was the SGEIS, which was supposed to guide the establishment of high-volume hydrofracking. I ended up giving presentations to many towns around upstate New York. Sometimes this was on my own or in a small group. Sometimes it was as part of panel discussions with people from both sides of the fracking debate.

Standing Room Only

A Canadian drilling company started drilling nearby, and that got people's attention. . . . And then they started doing some seismic testing in the town of Middlefield. When the seismic [testing] took place, [it] spurred a grassroots anti-fracking group to form almost overnight. It was mostly women. They started going to the town board. I own property in the town, so I went over, talked some. Another nearby town, Otsego, asked me to be on their gas advisory committee. So I did that. Once a month we'd get together. There were some pro-drillers on it, some anti. When it came to the town meetings, the town halls hardly ever had anybody come unless they needed a stop sign or some issue like that. And all of a sudden there was standing room only. And it just kind of kept building.

Those two town boards pretty quickly realized that they had to do something and started thinking about how they could zone it out [using zoning regulations to ban the industry from town limits, a strategy that has since been remarkably successful]. That was in the early days of talking about the possibility that you could indeed zone against drilling.

In the early days, I was not sure that a ban was the right thing to do. I was thinking that there probably could be a technical solution, and if you had regulations [written] properly, you might be able to do it. The industry had solved some huge technical problems over the years. Like, how do you drill 250 miles offshore in iceberg alley off Newfoundland?

More Fracking Consequences

The industry actually has a lot of very smart people working for it. As long as the box that they're working in is manageable, they can do a very good job. I think that what you've got in fracking is 'How do we work in a box this big,' narrowly defining the problem, [he holds his hands a foot apart in front of him] when you're really working in a huge box [he stretches his arms out wide]. The real box is as big as the

A Community Bans Fracking

In 2011, concerns over the environmental, health and business impacts of fracking, combined with a lack of federal guidance on the issue, led the towns of Middlefield and Otsego, which together encompass the village of Cooperstown, to pass the first local fracking bans by limiting industrial activities within the town's borders....

Since then, New York's local bans have been duplicated across the country.

Jessica A. Knoblauch,
"Fracking Runs Afoul of Hometown U.S.A.,"
Earthjustice Quarterly Magazine, *Fall 2012.*

globe and the atmosphere. And they're not seeing the consequences of moving outside the small box that they're working in.

So to go back to your earlier comments, what are the future consequences?

20, 30, 100 years down the road we don't know how much methane is going to be making its way up. And if you do hundreds of thousands of wells, there's a good chance you're going to have a lot of methane coming up, exacerbating global warming.... That is what Tony Ingraffea is talking about as part of the problem. [Anthony Ingraffea, Dwight C. Baum professor of engineering at Cornell University, in 2011 coauthored a landmark study on the greenhouse gas footprint of high-volume fracking.]

What you [also] don't know [is that] when you plug that well, how much is going to find its way to the surface without going up the wellbore. And there are lots of good indications that plugging the well doesn't really work long term. There's still some pressure down there even though it's not enough pressure to be commercially produced. And sooner or later the steel casing there is going to rust out, and the cement sooner or later is going to crumble. We may have better cements now, we may have slightly better techniques of packing the cement and mud into the wellbore to close it up, but even if nothing comes up through the fissures in the rock layers above, where it was fracked, those wellbores will deteriorate over time. And there is at least one study showing that 100 percent of plugs installed in abandoned wells fail within 100 years and many of them much sooner.

The Way Forward

So what's the solution?

I think we have wasted a lot of time that should have gone into seriously looking into and developing alternative energies. And we need to stop wasting that time and get going on it. But the difficult part is that the industry talks about, well, this is a bridge fuel [that] will carry us until alternatives [are developed] but nobody is building them. It's not a bridge unless you build the foundations for a bridge on the other side, and nobody's building it.

Have corporations like Mobil considered developing alternative energies?

Yes. Back after the first [1973] and second [1980] oil crises, when we had the spikes in prices and the lines and rationing, there was a lot of talk and substantial investments in alternative energies. Mobil invested in solar, and so did Exxon, and kept it going for quite a number of years. They abandoned it as just not coming up to the technical promises [because] solar cells weren't converting enough sun to electricity to be economically viable. There was also at that time a fair amount of work done on shale oil in the western states, and that was not fracking for shale. It was mining the shale and trying to extract oil from it. It just never came through. More recently there've been attempts at biofuels and some attempts to use algae.

Obama and the Future

What are your thoughts about President Obama's national address on climate change?

Well, when he talked about the [Keystone] XL pipeline he said he wanted to be sure it didn't increase carbon emissions. When he talks about natural gas, he kind of broad-brushes it and implies it's better than coal.

The whole speech is feeding into [ExxonMobil chief executive officer] Rex Tillerson's comments at a recent Exxon-Mobil shareholders' meeting where he said there's nothing we can do to switch to alternative fuels [and still] allow economies to continue the way they are. Society has to solve the problems by dealing with global warming—building levees around the cities, things like that. Obama is feeding into that, saying we have to strengthen the infrastructure. Basically what the industry is doing is unloading all the costs of what it's been doing onto the public. Just go out and build miles and miles of levees around New York City and build drainage systems and things like that. Obama is saying the same thing. We'll go on producing natural gas and keep the cost low by having the taxpayers pick up the cost of dealing with the consequences of global warming. Obama proposed some very positive steps toward developing alternative energies but he is not addressing the impact that methane has on global warming.

Fractivists and the Future

You've been on both sides now—promoting fossil fuel development for your whole life until your retirement and now trying to fight fracking. Do you think the anti-fracking movement and other environmental movements are the main hope now?

I think the main question is how fast can these movements educate enough people about the dangers of fracking and its impact on global warming. It will take masses of people demanding action from politicians to offset the huge amount of money that the industry is using to influence lawmakers, a world-scale version of those standing-room-only town meetings. Something has to wake up the general public. It will either be education from the environmental movements or some kind of climate disaster that no one can ignore.

| *"Total methane emissions from fracking are about 10 percent lower than levels set by EPA."*

Fracking Does Not Contribute to Global Warming

Coral Davenport

Coral Davenport is the energy and environmental reporter for National Journal. In the following viewpoint, Davenport explains that according to a study conducted by scientists at the University of Texas, the methane emissions produced by hydraulic fracturing are not sufficient to contribute negatively to climate change. It is probable that the study's findings will give ammunition to the government's efforts to increase regulation on coal-fired power plants, pointing to fracked natural gas as a cheaper and safer alternative, Davenport speculates.

As you read, consider the following questions:

1. What are the concerns of environmental groups regarding fracking that Davenport cites?

2. What conclusions did the study reach about methane emissions from fracking?

3. According to the viewpoint, how many sites in which areas were studied by the University of Texas researchers?

F rackers, rejoice.

A new study in the *Proceedings of the National Academy of Sciences* concludes that hydraulic fracturing—the controversial technique behind the nation's recent oil and gas boom—doesn't appear to contribute significantly to global warming, as many environmental groups have warned.

Good News for Oil and Gas Companies

It's great news for oil and gas companies such as ExxonMobil, Shell, and Chevron, which have relied on breakthroughs in so-called fracking technology to cheaply unlock vast new reserves of domestic oil and natural gas that had been trapped underground in shale-rock formations.

Hydraulic fracturing involves cracking open shale rock by injecting a cocktail of sand, water, and chemicals underground. Many environmental groups fear that the process can contaminate underground water supplies—and also that it releases underground stores of methane, a potent greenhouse gas that can have 20 times more impact on global warming than carbon dioxide.

"It's very good news," said Richard Keil, a spokesman for ExxonMobil, of the study. "This is a groundbreaking survey. It's the most extensive one that's been done yet, and it serves to add important new evidence that hydraulic fracturing does not contribute to climate change—it does not contribute methane emissions at levels higher than those set by the Environmental Protection Agency [EPA]."

The study is also good news for the [Barack] Obama administration, which is expected this week to release one in a series of new global warming regulations on coal-fired power plants, the nation's chief contributor to global warming. White House officials contend that the climate change rules aren't likely to hurt the economy, in part because the coal power can be replaced by the new glut of cheaply fracked natural gas, which produces just half the carbon pollution of coal. However, if fears that natural gas fracking contributed major greenhouse gas methane emissions proved true, it could have frozen the natural gas boom and made it far more difficult for the Obama White House to rein in climate pollution without seeing spikes in energy costs.

The White House and EPA [Environmental Protection Agency] "have expressed great interest in the findings," said David Allen, a professor of chemical engineering at the University of Texas and the lead author of the study. Allen has been invited to brief EPA and other administration officials on the research.

It's expected that the study's results could also be taken into account as EPA and the Interior Department look toward crafting new regulations on fracking.

"This is the first data ever collected from unconventional oil and gas development. With good data, you can make good policy," said Mark Brownstein, associate vice president and chief counsel for the Environmental Defense Fund's U.S. climate and energy program.

"People have rightly raised the issue—is natural gas better for the climate than coal or oil? This is a first step to getting better information to answer that question."

Fracking Releases Acceptable Levels of Methane

The study concluded that the majority of hydraulically fractured natural gas wells have surface equipment that reduces on-the-ground methane emissions by 99 percent, although it also found that elsewhere on fracking rigs, some valves do allow methane to escape at levels 30 percent higher than those set by EPA. Overall, however, the study concludes that total methane emissions from fracking are about 10 percent lower than levels set by EPA.

The $2.3 million study was conducted by scientists at the University of Texas, with funding provided by nine energy companies, including ExxonMobil, and one environmental group, the Environmental Defense Fund. A spokesman for the University of Texas said that while the companies contributed money to the study, they had no input on the research or results, which were subject to independent peer review before being published in the *Proceedings of the National Academy of Sciences*, one of the nation's most prestigious scientific journals.

A 2011 study by Cornell University researchers ignited opposition to fracking when it concluded that methane leaks from natural gas wells actually made natural gas a more climate-unfriendly energy source than coal. Although Obama has championed natural gas as a low-carbon "bridge" fuel to the future, green groups cited the Cornell study as reason that natural gas could become a climate nightmare.

University of Texas researchers say their yearlong study, which involved measuring methane emissions from 190 natural gas production sites in the Gulf coast, mid-continent, Rocky Mountains, and Appalachia, is far more comprehensive than the Cornell study, which relied on existing data rather than new fieldwork.

The study's authors and sponsors said that while the study is robust and comprehensive, more research on methane emissions along the natural gas supply chain is still needed. The Environmental Defense Fund intends to sponsor more than a dozen such studies in the coming years.

| *"The impact can be huge on particular communities and is 'exacerbating already existing water problems.'"*

Report: Fracking Raises Water Supply Worries

Julie Schmit

Julie Schmit is a reporter for USA Today. *In the following viewpoint, she states that a report from Ceres, a green investment group, says that fracking has required almost one hundred billion gallons of water to drill wells from 2011 to 2014 and that the majority of these wells are in areas with heavy water demands. While recycling water will help, most gas and oil companies are not yet doing this, she relates.*

As you read, consider the following questions:

1. What percentage of wells are in drought-stricken areas, and what percentage are in areas under high water stress, according to the Ceres report?

2. What percentage of the total water demand do oil and gas account for in Colorado and Texas?

3. According to the viewpoint, what percentage of water used for fracking in Texas is recycled?

The USA's domestic energy boom is increasing demands on water supplies already under pressure from drought and growing populations, a new report says.

The water-intensive process used to extract oil and gas from shale underground—known as hydraulic fracturing or fracking—has required almost 100 billion gallons of water to drill more than 39,000 oil and shale gas wells in the U.S. since 2011, says Ceres, a green investment group.

More than half of those wells—55%—were in drought-stricken areas, and nearly half were in regions under high or extremely high water stress, such as Texas, the report says.

Fracking Places Demands on Water Supplies

To be in extremely high water stress means more than 80% of the area's available surface and groundwater is already allocated for city, agriculture or industrial use. High stress means 40% to 80% of the water is already allocated, Ceres says.

Shale development is also occurring rapidly in areas where groundwater is already being depleted by other uses, including agriculture and residential development.

Nationwide, more than 36% of the 39,000 wells drilled since 2011 were in areas already experiencing groundwater depletion, the study says.

Hydraulic fracturing pumps water and chemicals at high pressure to break the shale, allowing trapped oil or gas to flow to the surface.

While fracking consumes far less water than agriculture or residential uses, the impact can be huge on particular communities and is "exacerbating already existing water problems," says Monika Freyman, author of the Ceres study.

Fracking Escalates Demand for Water

Future water demand for hydraulic fracturing will only grow with tens of thousands of additional wells slated to be drilled, and many shale basins and plays are just beginning to be developed. In addition, the shale development business model requires continual drilling cycles to maintain production growth.

All across the country, regulators, producers and service providers are scrambling to find technological and regulatory solutions to mitigate localized water-sourcing risks from rapid shale energy development. Some pockets of success can be found. Apache [Corporation], for example, is recycling 100 percent of produced water in the Permian Basin. Anadarko [Petroleum Corporation] and Shell [formally known as Royal Dutch Shell] are buying effluent water from local municipalities. Chesapeake [Energy] is reusing nearly 100 percent of its produced water and drilling wastewater in the Marcellus region.

Viewed more widely, however, water management best practices are lagging and no single technology alone—whether recycling, brackish water use or greater use of waterless hydraulic fracturing technology—will solve regional water sourcing and water stress problems. Ultimately, all shale operators and service providers should be deploying a variety of tools and strategies— including substantially improved operational practices related to water sourcing, more robust stakeholder engagement and stronger disclosure—to protect freshwater resources for the future.

Monika Freyman,
"Hydraulic Fracturing and Water Stress:
Water Demand by the Numbers," February 2014.

Hydraulic fracking is the "latest party to come to the table," Freyman says. The demands for the water are also "taking regions by surprise," she says. More work needs to be done to better manage water use, given competing demands, she says.

Texas has the highest concentration of hydraulic fracturing activity in the U.S. More than half of its wells put in since 2011 were in high or extremely high water stress regions, Ceres says.

In Colorado and California, 97% and 96% respectively of the wells were drilled in regions under high or extremely high water stress.

The oil and gas industry says it's doing more to reuse and recycle water. It also points out that overall water use by the fracking industry is small.

In Colorado, oil and gas development accounts for 0.1% of the state's total water demand, while in Texas, it's less than 1%, says Katie Brown, researcher with Energy in Depth, a research arm of the Independent Petroleum Association of America.

A recent report from the University of Texas also found that natural gas fracking saves water overall by making it easier for utilities to switch from coal to natural gas power. As a result, it's helping to "shield the state from water shortages," Brown says.

More recycling will occur because companies "recognize the economic risk they have," with access to needed water, says Marcus Gay, water research director at IHS Global Insight.

Only about 5% of water consumed by oil and gas producers in the Barnett Shale in North Texas is currently being recycled, says a recent report by research scientist Jean-Philippe Nicot, of the University of Texas. That's probably about average for fracking throughout Texas, Nicot says.

Producers in Pennsylvania, meanwhile, are doing more recycling because they lack good access to deep injection wells to store spent water. For those companies, "it's cheaper to recycle" than ship the water out of state to deep injection wells, Nicot says.

| "*The oil and natural gas industry's water risk is actually 'low to medium' over the vast majority of the United States.*"

Fracking Does Not Harm the Water Supply

Energy in Depth

In the following viewpoint, Energy in Depth (EID) argues that the Ceres report, which warns that fracking is placing significant water demands on regions already under high water stress, is deliberately misleading. The viewpoint points out that Ceres is not an objective organization but rather one composed of environmental activist groups. Furthermore, EID argues, Ceres concealed from the public data from the World Resources Institute that showed that the oil and gas industry's water risk is actually low to medium over most of the United States.

As you read, consider the following questions:

1. How does the water risk of oil and natural gas compare to industries such as construction, electric power, agriculture, textiles, and food and beverage, according to the viewpoint?

2. According to the viewpoint, what percentage of the water use in Colorado and Pennsylvania is devoted to fracking?

3. In what ways does the author report that fracking is helping to reduce the amount of water needed for oil and natural gas development overall?

A Boston-based group called Ceres made national and international headlines this week [February 7, 2014] by claiming hydraulic fracturing has put the oil and natural gas industry on a "collision course" with other water users in some of America's driest states.

The Ceres Report Is Misleading

But the group's latest report [*Hydraulic Fracturing and Water Stress: Water Demand by the Numbers*] is highly misleading and concealed key data from the news media and the public showing much smaller water impacts from oil and natural gas operations. The report also presents Ceres as a nonprofit concerned with protecting investors in oil and natural gas companies, when its membership includes environmental activist groups that openly oppose oil and natural gas production.

The recent report builds on a 2013 Ceres paper based on the "Aqueduct" mapping tool of the World Resources Institute [WRI]. According to a Ceres press release, the WRI data shows "nearly half" of the wells fractured between Jan. 2011 and May 2013 "were in regions with high or extremely high water stress." Ceres claims this creates "significant long-term water sourcing risks for [oil and natural gas] companies operating in these regions as well as their investors," and puts the industry on a "collision course with other water users."

But despite the best efforts of Ceres to portray water consumption as a high or extremely high risk to the oil and natural gas industry, the WRI data tell a much different story. What Ceres concealed from the public was WRI's own measure of "overall water risk" for the oil and gas industry. . . . [The] oil and natural gas industry's water risk is actually "low to medium" over the vast majority of the United States, and only a few areas of "medium to high" risk. . . .

Even more telling, the WRI data show the oil and natural gas industry's overall water risk is relatively low compared to every other sector examined. . . . [Oil] and natural gas have a much lower water risk than construction, electric power, agriculture, textiles, food and beverage and other industries. . . .

In fact, it appears *oil and natural gas development has the lowest water risk of all the industries* examined by WRI. But how is this possible when so much oil and natural gas production occurs in dry states?

The average hydraulic fracturing job uses an average of four million gallons of water, depending on location and geology. While that seems like a large number, it's important to put it into context. Four million gallons of water is approximately:

- The amount that is emptied from the Mississippi River into the Gulf of Mexico *every second*.

- The amount of water New York City consumes *every six minutes*.

- About 1.3 percent of the amount of water used in car washes every day.

- The amount of water just one of the 15,889 golf courses across the United States uses in less than one summer month.

The Environmental Protection Agency (EPA) estimates "approximately 400 billion gallons of water are used in the United States per day." According to Ceres' water use estimates, the roughly 97 billion gallons of water used for hydraulic fracturing across the United States from January 2011 to May 2013—a period of more than two years—is less than one-quarter the amount of water used in the United States *in a single day.*

As Ceres itself notes, "hydraulic fracturing is largely taking place in regions already experiencing high competition for water." In Colorado, the oil and natural gas industry used roughly 6.5 billion gallons of water in 2012. That's a lot of water—but only 0.1 percent of the state's overall water use. Agriculture and irrigation are two of the largest users, consuming 85.5 percent of the state's supply. Same goes for Pennsylvania, where a report by Accenture found of the 3.6 trillion gallons of water consumed by the state annually, "the shale gas industry uses less than 0.2% of that for hydraulic fracturing."

In fact, the Environmental Protection Agency estimates landscape irrigation consumes roughly three trillion gallons a year. According to the *Wall Street Journal,* that's "*more than 20 times its highest estimate for the amount of water used annually in fracking.*"

The oil and natural gas industry is also investing and innovating to reduce its water use. As the Bureau of Economic Geology at the University of Texas found, about one-fifth of the water used in hydraulic fracturing in Texas is recycled or brackish water, thanks to efforts from various producers. In the Permian Basin, Apache [Corporation] has increased its use of brackish water from the Santa Rosa aquifer as well as produced water, largely eliminating the need for freshwater.

Halliburton Co., one of the largest providers of hydraulic fracturing services across the globe, is using more recycled water and seawater, which means reduced consumption of freshwater, and has set a goal for industry to use an average of 25 percent less freshwater in hydraulic fracturing by the end of 2014. As Ceres even notes, "Anadarko [Petroleum Corporation] and Shell [formally known as Royal Dutch Shell] are buying effluent water from local municipalities. Chesapeake

[Energy] is reusing nearly 100 percent of its produced water and drilling wastewater in the Marcellus region."

Some reports have actually found hydraulic fracturing is ultimately *helping to reduce the amount of water* needed for oil and natural gas development overall. A recent study by researchers at Kent State and Duke University found the use of hydraulic fracturing in the Marcellus shale actually requires less water per unit of energy than conventional wells. In Texas, Bridget Scanlon, senior research scientist at the University of Texas's Bureau of Economic Geology, stated that hydraulic fracturing is actually making the state more "drought resilient" by "boosting natural gas production and moving the state" away from more water-intensive energy uses.

Activists or Investors?

While the Ceres coalition does include some institutional investors—mostly public-employee pension funds—it also has a large number of activist groups that actively oppose the oil and natural gas industry, a fact you won't find disclosed in the Ceres report. Check out EID's [Energy in Depth's] earlier post on Ceres to see what many of these members—including the Sierra Club, Friends of the Earth, Natural Resources Defense Council, American Rivers and others—have said about oil and natural gas development, including hydraulic fracturing specifically.

Besides these members, Ceres also has many donors—and you may or may not be surprised to learn that they include some well-known funders of anti-fracking activism. According to the group's last annual report, those donors include the Park Foundation, the Energy Foundation, the Tides Foundation, and the Rockefeller Brothers Fund. But again, that's something you won't find disclosed in this report on hydraulic fracturing.

Water use is a serious issue across many states that should be a priority and a concern for communities and businesses alike. That's why the oil and natural gas industry is continually innovating to reduce its water use impacts, enhance recycling, and use other non-freshwater sources. Unfortunately, Ceres largely ignores that reality and instead distorts facts and figures to create a false narrative that intends to invoke blame on hydraulic fracturing for America's water stress—no doubt because many of its members and donors want them to say that.

The facts, however, tell a different story.

Periodical and Internet Sources Bibliography

The following articles have been selected to supplement the diverse views presented in this chapter.

Ronald Bailey	"Natural Gas Flip-Flop: Big Environmental Groups Were for Fracking Before They Were Against It," *Reason*, August–September 2011.
Colin Barras	"Fracking Hell," *New Scientist*, December 14, 2013.
Abrahm Lustgarten and Nick Kusnetz	"Feds Link Water Contamination to Fracking for the First Time," ProPublica, December 8, 2011.
Andrew Marantz	"Underfoot," *New Yorker*, November 25, 2013.
Marita Noon	"The Secret Danger Liberals Don't Want You to Know: Fracking Is Safe," Townhall.com, December 29, 2013.
John Simaz	"Debunking a Year's Worth of Falsehoods from Ban Michigan Fracking," Energy in Depth Michigan, January 17, 2014.
Mark Venables	"Fracking Protestors Should Focus on the More Pressing Issues," *Energy & Technology*, October 2013.
Bryan Walsh	"The Golden Age: Could Europe and China's Fracking Forays Remake Global Energy?," *Time*, May 21, 2012.
Alyson Warhit	"Study: Fracking May Be More Harmful than Coal Use," *Cornell Daily Sun*, April 18, 2011.
Fareed Zakaria	"Shale Gas, an Alternative to Oil That Is Bolstering the U.S. Economy," *Washington Post*, March 29, 2012.

CHAPTER 2

Does the United States Need More Gas Pipeline Capacity?

Chapter Preface

On March 12, 2014, a gas leak caused an explosion that killed eight people and injured more than sixty others in two adjacent apartment buildings in New York City's East Harlem. Sadly, the explosion was not an isolated incident—in 2011 a gas leak in Allentown, Pennsylvania, killed five people, and in 2010 a rupture in a San Bruno, California, pipeline caused an explosion that killed eight.

As investigators searched for the causes of these tragedies, a pattern emerged. The early stages of the investigation into the Harlem explosion indicated that a 127-year-old cast-iron pipe serving the apartments most likely leaked due to cracking or corrosion. A leaky 83-year-old cast-iron pipeline was identified by the Pennsylvania Public Utility Commission as the cause of the Allentown explosion. The pipeline in the San Bruno explosion was more than fifty years old and had been inadequately welded, leading to a rupture when an electrical problem released large quantities of gas into the line. With each of these tragedies caused by aging pipeline infrastructure, safety experts are concerned, since more than 60 percent of all US natural gas pipelines were installed before 1970, and 37 percent are from the 1950s or earlier.

The question of what to do to make this infrastructure safer in an affordable way is an issue that communities across the United States have been grappling with. Allentown mayor Ed Pawlowski would like more replacement of the old cast-iron pipelines. "We are going to see more and more about these kinds of tragedies until we get serious about how do we regulate and replace these lines," he was quoted as saying in the *Allentown Morning Call*.

Others cite the replacement of all old pipelines as cost prohibitive and recommend repair and better monitoring practices as a more practical solution. To replace all of the old

As you read, consider the following questions:

1. According to Smith, from where does the Northeast get most of its electric energy output?

2. What gasoline projects does the author deem worth noting?

3. Why is natural gas consumption predicted to increase substantially over the next few decades, according to the viewpoint?

Reducing energy costs for New Hampshire businesses is critical to increasing their competitive position in the region and beyond. Natural gas could be a significant part of the answer.

Last year [2012], New England's wholesale electricity prices fell by nearly 23 percent, partly as a result of low natural gas prices. More than half of New England's electric energy output is now being generated from natural gas and, with recent discoveries of large domestic shale gas deposits in Pennsylvania, Ohio and West Virginia, there is potential for even more savings. As coal plants are retired and oil prices skyrocket, natural gas will likely continue to bring some needed relief to New Hampshire businesses burdened by historically high energy costs.

The question is: How much relief?

Plans for Additional Pipelines

With five interstate gas pipelines serving New England, New Hampshire appears well positioned to take greater advantage of this plentiful, less costly and cleaner-burning fuel. Yet ISO New England's [ISO-NE] president recently told the U.S. Senate Energy and Natural Resources Committee that pipeline constraints for the region's electric generators may prevent us from taking full advantage of shale gas deposits to the west and south. ISO-NE predicted that until additional pipeline capacity is built in the region, price spikes from constrained capacity—similar to those experienced this past winter [of 2013]—would likely continue.

Even though New England's electricity market design does not currently provide appropriate incentives for gas generators to make the long-term, firm commitments required for pipeline infrastructure investments—a problem that ISO-NE acknowledges and is trying to remedy—interstate pipeline companies still appear willing to take the plunge toward expanding capacity into the region at the same time that restructured power markets continue to develop and expand.

Several projects worth watching include recent proposals by Spectra Energy, Tennessee Gas Pipeline Company (TGPL) and Portland Natural Gas Transmission System (PNGTS). The proposals would expand existing natural gas pipelines and increase incremental capacity deeper into the region and into New Hampshire.

Because the new capacity would create the potential for expanding local natural gas distribution directly to businesses, along with more reliable supplies to electric generators, New Hampshire's industrial and commercial sectors will want to pay close attention to their progress.

Spectra, which operates the Algonquin Gas Transmission pipeline system, is in the early planning phase of the proposed Algonquin Incremental Market (AIM) Project. The existing pipeline brings western and southern natural gas supplies to New Jersey, New York, Connecticut and Massachusetts. The expansion would follow the path of the existing pipeline but would increase capacity by 20–25 percent, with a slated expansion capacity of 450,000 dekatherms per day starting in 2016.

The AIM Project is expected to ease natural gas capacity constraints in the region, helping to reduce the risk of regional price spikes. An open season is under way to allow for firm service requests from interested parties.

> *"The region is getting closer and closer to the winter morning when there's not enough gas to keep the lights on and buildings warm."*

More Natural Gas Pipeline Capacity Is Needed

Peter Howe

Peter Howe is the business editor for New England Cable News (NECN). In the following viewpoint, Howe reports that with the Northeast facing a natural gas shortage in periods of peak usage due to insufficient pipeline capacity, all six New England governors support a tax on electricity to pay for more pipelines. Because an increased supply of gas could lower its price, it is possible that a pipeline expansion would be cost effective and affordable, he suggests.

As you read, consider the following questions:

1. What reasoning does the author use to support his contention that pipeline expansion in New England could pay for itself?

2. What are some of the arguments that environmentalists have against a tax to support pipeline expansion, according to Howe?

3. According to the viewpoint, what are the concerns of power plant owners regarding pipeline expansion?

With more and more New England homes and businesses heating with natural gas, and more and more of the region's electricity coming each year from natural-gas-fired power plants—but no new pipelines—the region is getting closer and closer to the winter morning when there's not enough gas to keep the lights on and buildings warm.

New England Governors Support a Tax for Increased Pipeline Capacity

"What we're seeing is recurring shortages of natural gas coming up to the region, particularly during winter months when gas usage is really, really high," Robert Rio, vice president and energy expert at Associated Industries of Massachusetts [AIM], the state's biggest business lobbying group, said in an interview Monday [January 27, 2014] afternoon. "We really do need more pipeline capacity."

That's an assessment all six New England governors share, and in a letter to power grid operator ISO New England late last week, they said they'd be willing to back a new wholesale tax on electricity—or "tariff"—to pay for it.

Spectra Energy's Algonquin pipeline unit has announced plans for a project—estimated to cost $500 million or more—to add 26 miles of new pipeline and increased pumping capacity to add about 7.8 percent more incoming gas capacity to the regional pipeline network.

The governors said they want ISO New England to push for the equivalent of a 17.8 percent increase, or an extra 1 billion cubic feet per day of capacity on a network a 2012 Black & Veatch study said can bring 5.6 billion cubic feet of gas a day into New England.

Currently, the region is supplied by five pipeline systems bringing gas produced in Canada, the Gulf of Mexico, and the growing shale fields of Pennsylvania and Ohio and neighboring states, along with three liquefied natural gas terminals in and off the coast of Boston.

What no one has offered is any kind of price tag for what the governors want, or how much it would add to homeowners' and businesses' electric bills.

But to take a round number, a $1 billion investment in new pipeline capacity paid for with 20-year bonds bearing a current typical corporate rate of 4.5 percent would cost $75 million a year for 20 years. Given that New England spends $10 billion a year for electricity, that wouldn't add even 1 percent to the overall electric bill. And some energy experts argue that an increase in supply could lower the wholesale price of natural gas in New England and thus lower the cost of electric generation, so a pipeline expansion could, in fact, more than pay for itself in lower household and business electric rates.

Why more pipeline companies haven't lined up to propose more expansions of the network to help New England tap cheap, abundant gas to the west—and the extent to which they maximize profits by the current supply capacity constraints—is far from clear.

Environmentalists Oppose Pipeline Tax

Environmentalists like the Conservation Law Foundation's Seth L. Kaplan are dubious about the governors' pipeline appeal, on legal, process, and climate change grounds.

"ISO New England collecting money from electric customers to pay for gas pipelines is at least at the limits—if not beyond the limits—of their legal authority," Kaplan said.

Governors Underestimated Pipeline Need

There has been a fundamental shift in the New England natural gas market since 2012 that is causing price spikes during winter months to be much higher and more frequent than they have previously been. As a result, studies of the natural gas market that were done prior to the winter 2012/2013 or that rely on data prior to that period will understate significantly the financial consequences of inadequate natural gas pipeline capacity into New England.

1 bcf/d [billion cubic feet per day] of additional pipeline capacity into the region, as proposed in the recent governors' letter, will provide partial relief to the region from high natural gas and electricity prices but will not eliminate the basis differential between New England and pricing points to our west and south.

2 bcf/d of additional pipeline capacity is required to eliminate the natural gas price differential between New England and pricing points to the region's west and south.

Competitive Energy Services,
"Assessing Natural Gas Supply Options for New England
and Their Impacts on Natural Gas and Electricity Prices,"
February 7, 2014.

Kaplan also said scientific analysis of global climate change shows rather than investing in more gas pipelines, "In the near future, we are going to have to get off all fossil fuels, including natural gas. . . . We need to be off natural gas and all fossil fuels at some point before the middle of this century" to avoid catastrophic planetary climate change.

He also complained that the discussions that led to the January 21 letter from the New England States Committee on Electricity "were far from open and transparent," and more groups and viewpoints need to have their voices and concerns heard before ISO New England and governors move to increase power capacity.

Also concerned are power plant owners, who fear the move could distort the wholesale power markets.

Dan Dolan, president of the New England Power Generators Association, said, "I have concerns about the states picking winners and losers in the marketplace. Natural gas is a critical part of our electricity marketplace and will be for some time. More pipelines could certainly help provide fuel for power generation, but there are already multiple competing pipelines to come into the region. I'm not sure there is a need for this type of extraordinary role for consumers to subsidize infrastructure. We are unfortunately in a gap period where the electricity market has responded to historically low natural gas prices by moving aggressively in that direction and the fuel delivery infrastructure is catching up. My guess is we start seeing new pipelines come online by 2017, which will dramatically improve the situation."

Business and government leaders' immediate concern is keeping the heat and lights on, and at a price that doesn't ravage economic growth.

Massachusetts Energy and Environmental Affairs spokeswoman Mary-Leah Assad said the pipeline capacity issue has been paired with a push for more transmission capacity to bring renewable energy and Canadian hydropower into the region.

"Massachusetts and the other New England states sit at the end of the energy pipeline, making the energy we use more expensive for our residents and businesses. In an effort to reduce these costs and ensure an adequate supply of clean energy and natural gas, the New England governors are working together to increase transmission to the region," Assad said. "Through this partnership, the governors aim to build transmission infrastructure to deliver as much as 3,600 megawatts of electricity from clean energy sources into the grid, and to develop a funding mechanism to support investment in pipelines that bring natural gas into the region."

AIM's Rio said his association is still studying the governors' letter and developing a response.

"We all agree, I think, that New England is lacking in natural gas pipeline capacity," he said.

"*American consumers, businesses and communities now pay for gas they don't receive and bear the risks of gas leaks they cannot repair.*"

Leaky Gas Pipelines Cost Consumers Billions

US House of Representatives Natural Resources Committee Democratic Staff

The US House of Representatives Natural Resources Committee oversees the nation's energy and mineral resources, fisheries, wildlife, oceans, public lands, environmental regulations, and water and power. In the following viewpoint, the committee contends that although natural gas is considered a cleaner alternative than coal as a source of electricity, aging pipelines leaking methane gas into the atmosphere negate many of its benefits. Gas distribution companies have little incentive to repair leaky pipelines because they are able to pass along the cost of the lost gas to consumers, the committee claims. Legislation is needed to ensure that gas companies are accountable for these leaks, the committee concludes.

As you read, consider the following questions:

1. According to the viewpoint, how much have consumers paid for lost gas from 2000–2011?

"America Pays for Gas Leaks," a report prepared for Senator Edward J. Markey, August 1, 2013, US House of Representatives Natural Resources Committee Democratic Staff.

2. What steps does the committee recommend to resolve the problem of methane emissions in Massachusetts?

3. What steps does the committee recommend to accelerate pipeline replacement?

A merican consumers are paying billions of dollars for natural gas that never reaches their homes, but instead leaks from aging distribution pipelines, contributing to climate change, threatening public health, and sometimes causing explosions. This staff report, which was prepared at the request of Sen. Edward J. Markey (D-MA), draws on data from a variety of sources to assess the impact of leaks and other "lost and unaccounted for" natural gas, using Massachusetts as a case study.

Gas Companies Have Little Incentive to Fix Leaks

Gas distribution companies in 2011 reported releasing 69 billion cubic feet of natural gas to the atmosphere, almost enough to meet the state of Maine's gas needs for a year and equal to the annual carbon dioxide emissions of about six million automobiles. Nonetheless, last year [2012] these companies replaced just 3 percent of their distribution mains made of cast iron or bare steel, which leak 18 times more gas than plastic pipes and 57 times more gas than protected steel. Gas companies have little incentive to replace these leaky pipes, which span about 91,000 miles across 46 states, because they are able to pass along the cost of lost gas to consumers. Nationally, consumers paid at least $20 billion from 2000–2011 for gas that was unaccounted for and never used, according to analysis performed for this report.

Natural gas has been touted as a cleaner alternative to coal for producing electricity, but its environmental benefits cannot be fully realized so long as distribution pipelines are leaking such enormous quantities of gas, which is primarily comprised of methane, a greenhouse gas that is at least 21 times more potent than carbon dioxide. Americans also remain at risk from gas explosions and other safety hazards caused by leaky natural gas pipelines. From 2002 to 2012, almost 800 significant incidents on gas distribution pipelines, including several hundred explosions, killed 116 people, injured 465 others, and caused more than $800 million in property damage.

Gov. Deval Patrick's administration has started to address this problem in Massachusetts, which is a nationally recognized leader among states in energy efficiency and reducing greenhouse gas emissions. In particular, the commonwealth's Department of Public Utilities (DPU) recently launched incentive programs to encourage gas companies to replace leak-prone pipelines and operate more efficiently. The incentive programs are needed because gas companies in Massachusetts own and operate one of America's oldest natural gas pipeline distribution systems, ranking sixth among state systems in the number of miles of main distribution pipelines made of cast iron or bare steel. These companies have replaced less than 4 percent of their leak-prone pipes per year while billing Massachusetts ratepayers an estimated $640 million to $1.5 billion from 2000–2011 for unaccounted for gas.

The problem of leaky gas pipelines may be even worse than the data presented in this report suggests. Indeed, companies frequently report negative volumes of unaccounted for gas to various agencies—even though it's physically impossible to dispose of more gas than enters a closed system. Federal and state regulators explained in interviews for this report that there isn't a consistent methodology for calculating lost and unaccounted for gas, and data quality problems are common. . . .

Last year, 24.5 trillion cubic feet of natural gas was produced in the United States, up 4 trillion cubic feet [tcf] since 2007. Sales of natural gas from federal lands were about 18 percent (4.3 tcf) of total U.S. sales in fiscal year 2012, including 3 trillion cubic feet produced onshore and 1.3 trillion cubic feet produced offshore. Additionally, about 28 percent (85 tcf of 305 tcf) of U.S. proved reserves of dry natural gas are located on federal lands. Fixing leaky pipelines is important in making sure these newly abundant natural gas resources are put to responsible use and fully benefit the American people.

To address the problems identified in this report, Sen. Markey is drafting legislation that will push states and non-regulated utilities to accelerate replacement of high-risk, leaky pipelines and curtail the practice of passing along the costs of lost gas to consumers. The following section of the report uses Massachusetts as a case study to show why this legislation is necessary.

The Price of Leaked Gas

By not replacing leaking pipelines, gas companies nationwide are charging ratepayers for gas that never reaches homes and is contributing to climate change, endangering public health, and risking explosions and other safety hazards. The problem is particularly acute in Massachusetts because of the advanced age of the commonwealth's distribution system. Specifically, the data show:

- *Massachusetts ratepayers paid between $640 million to $1.5 billion from 2000–2011 for gas that never reached their homes and businesses.* At least 99 billion cubic feet of natural gas was "lost and unaccounted for" in Massachusetts from 2000–2011, according to data reported by utilities to the Massachusetts Department of Public Utilities (DPU). The cost of this unaccounted for gas—$640 million to $1.5 billion, according to calculations performed for this report—was passed on to the commonwealth's approximately 1.5 million residential, commercial and other customers.

- *Lost natural gas accounts for at least 45 percent of Massachusetts' methane emissions for large, stationary facilities.* Utilities serving Massachusetts reported releasing between 1.1 and 1.4 billion cubic feet of gas into the atmosphere in 2011, accounting for between 45 and 58 percent of the commonwealth's methane emissions for large, stationary facilities, as reported to the Massachusetts Greenhouse Gas Registry. . . .

- State law requires Massachusetts to reduce greenhouse gas emissions to 25 percent below 1990 levels by 2020. Addressing gas leaks is especially important in meeting this goal because methane is such a potent heat-trapping gas, with at least 21 times the warming potential of carbon dioxide over a 100-year time horizon and as much as 72 times the warming potential over a 20-year horizon. By 2010, Massachusetts had already succeeded in reducing methane emissions from the natural gas distribution system by 14 percent below 1990 levels.

- However, greater reductions are still possible by accelerating replacement of leaky pipes. Natural gas companies could reduce their emissions in Massachusetts to 25 percent below 1990 levels by replacing about 777 miles of cast-iron mains (the most leak-prone pipe material), according to staff calculations.

- Nationwide, the natural gas distribution system is the largest source of methane emissions, accounting for 19 percent of total emissions in 2011, according to the U.S. Environmental Protection Agency (EPA). EPA also found that recent reductions in U.S. methane emissions have been driven in part by replacing leak-prone pipelines in distribution systems.

- *More significant pipeline incidents in Massachusetts involved cast-iron or other high-risk pipes.* Incidents are four times more likely to occur on cast-iron mains than mains made of other materials, according to an analysis of national pipeline incidents by the U.S Pipeline and Hazardous Materials Safety Administration (PHMSA).

- In Massachusetts, 57 percent of the significant incidents from 2002–2012—attributable to human error, leaks, natural forces, excavation damage, and a variety of other causes—occurred around segments of the distribution system utilizing cast-iron or steel pipe. One of these incidents, a gas explosion in July 2002 involving a corroded fitting on a steel pipe, leveled a home and killed two children in Hopkinton, Mass. Another powerful explosion occurred in Springfield, Mass., last November, as a result of human error after a worker from Columbia Gas of Massachusetts accidently punctured a steel service line, which had been retrofitted with plastic, while responding to a call about a gas leak. The incident resulted in injuries to 17 people and $1.3 million in property damage, according PHMSA data.

- Nationally, a number of recent killer pipeline explosions have been traced to aging, cast-iron pipelines, including explosions in Austin, Texas, Philadelphia, and Allentown, Penn., where a gas main explosion in February 2011 resulted in five fatalities, three hospitalizations, and eight destroyed homes. Some of these accidents might have been prevented had gas companies performed timelier repair, rehabilitation and replacement of high-risk pipeline, such as cast-iron and unprotected bare steel pipes, according to PHMSA. PHMSA warns that "public safety requires prompt action [by gas companies] to repair, remediate, and replace high-risk gas pipeline infrastructure."

The Slow Pace of Fixing Leaks

There are some federal and state incentives in place to accelerate the pace of infrastructure replacement. Massachusetts is

US Unaccounted for Gas, Emissions, and Significant Incidents on Natural Gas Systems

Total US Unaccounted for Gas from Natural Gas Systems from 2000–2011	2.6 trillion cubic feet of natural gas
Total US Reported Emissions from Natural Gas Distribution Systems from 2010–2011	Equivalent to releasing 56.2 million metric tons of CO_2
Significant Incidents on US Natural Gas Distribution Systems from 2002–2012	796 incidents / 116 fatalities / 465 injuries / $810,677,757 in property damage

TAKEN FROM: US House of Representatives Natural Resources Committee Democratic Staff, "America Pays for Gas Leaks," August 1, 2013.

one of several forward-looking states that have either established or are considering policies that create financial incentives for gas companies to repair or replace leaky infrastructure. Despite these incentives, gas distribution companies' progress at replacing leak-prone pipeline remains slow. Specifically, the data show:

- *U.S. gas companies are replacing less than 5 percent of their leakiest pipes per year.* Cast iron and bare steel are the most leak-prone pipe materials, releasing 27.25 and 12.58 cubic feet of methane per hour, per mile, respectively, according to the EPA. PHMSA also lists these materials as high-risk pipeline infrastructure that is prone to failure. Nonetheless, last year gas companies nationwide replaced just 3 percent of their cast-iron and bare steel distribution mains—pipes that connect transmission lines to service lines—with less leak-prone plastic pipes. . . .

- *Nationwide, there are few federal or state incentives to repair or replace leaky pipes or minimize lost gas.* Federal pipeline safety regulations require only "hazardous leaks" posing imminent threat to be repaired promptly, allowing nonhazardous leaks to go unrepaired. Gas companies are required to identify and classify leaks according to risk as part of their federally mandated distribution integrity management plans, but only five states require all nonhazardous leaks to be repaired within a certain time frame. . . .

- *It's hard to monitor company performance because data on unaccounted for gas is of such poor quality.* Companies regularly report negative volumes of unaccounted for gas, and there can be substantial variance in the numbers reported across agencies. Negative unaccounted for gas volumes indicate calculating or reporting errors because it's physically impossible to dispose of more gas than enters a closed distribution system, according to a 2012 report prepared for the Pennsylvania [Public] Utility Commission. This report also noted that inconsistencies in methodologies across companies can inhibit regulators' ability to monitor company performance over time.

- According to federal and state officials, companies do not use a consistent methodology to calculate unaccounted for gas. Officials from PHMSA's Office of Pipeline Safety explained in an interview for this report that the agency provides companies with a formula for calculating unaccounted for gas, as well as guidance about the types of adjustments that are appropriate to make; however, each company decides which adjustments to make and less sophisticated operators may not make basic adjustments, such as adjusting volumes based on standard temperature pressure. . . .

Actions Needed to Accelerate Pipeline Replacement

Despite slow progress to date, some state initiatives—like those established or proposed in Massachusetts—show promise and should be expanded to accelerate the repair or replacement of leak-prone pipelines. In particular:

- *States and nonregulated utilities such as municipal gas companies should adopt cost recovery programs for accelerated replacement of high-risk, leak-prone pipelines.* Companies typically cannot recover the costs of their infrastructure investments until the utility files for and receives such approval, which can be many months—and sometimes more than a year—after costs have been incurred. Cost-recovery programs allow gas companies to recover the costs of infrastructure improvements on a timelier basis, which could provide more incentive for companies to replace their leaky pipelines. Ratepayers and the public may also benefit from these programs through increased safety, reductions in rates from decreased operations and maintenance and unaccounted for gas costs, and reduced greenhouse gas emissions, according to a recent analysis of such programs in New England.

- Taking into account widely accepted assumptions from the EPA regarding the rate of gas leaks, global warming potential and the social cost of carbon, and including costs associated with replacing pipelines, Massachusetts residents stand to realize $156 million in net benefits over 10 years from the companies participating in the commonwealth's infrastructure replacement program. One of these companies, Colonial Gas, increased their annual replacement rate of leak-prone pipeline by an average of 7 percent for service lines and 13 percent for main lines during its two years in the program. The other companies participating in the cost recovery program—Boston Gas, New England Gas, and Columbia Gas—have not appreciably improved their replacement rates of leak-prone pipes. This suggests that additional financial incentives, such as those currently under consideration by the Massachusetts legislature, may be needed. . . .

- *States and nonregulated utilities should establish time frames for repairing nonhazardous gas leaks.* Gas companies are already required by federal reputation to identify, classify, and manage safety risks posed by leaks. Nonetheless, leaks that do not pose a safety risk may continue unabated. Just five states—Florida, Georgia, Kansas, Maine and Texas—have established firm time frames for repairing all nonhazardous leaks, with time frames ranging from 3 months to 36 months for the least hazardous leaks. As noted by the Conservation Law Foundation, this program may be having an effect, as Maine had one of the lowest lost gas rates in the country, according to data from the Energy Information Administration. The Massachusetts legislature is considering repair time frames for all nonhazardous leaks.

- *States and nonregulated utilities should adopt a standard definition and methodology for calculating unaccounted for gas.* Inconsistent data reported by companies inhibits regulators' ability to perform oversight, according to the Pennsylvania Public Utility Commission and others. Furthermore, negative unaccounted for gas levels are indicative of calculating or reporting discrepancies, not actual gas volumes—and PHMSA does not allow companies to report negative values. To address this issue, the Pennsylvania commission adopted a standard definition and methodology for unaccounted for gas, based in part on PHMSA's definition. Other states with similar reporting issues should follow Pennsylvania's lead. Massachusetts state regulators plan to study the issue.

- *States and nonregulated utilities should limit the ability of gas companies to recover costs for unaccounted for gas.* Limiting the amount of unaccounted for gas for which companies can charge would create a powerful financial incentive for gas companies to minimize emissions. As noted earlier, Pennsylvania and Texas are the only states that have set statewide caps on the percentages of gas for which companies can recover costs. In both states, companies can recover costs for no more than 5 percent of the unaccounted for gas, and Pennsylvania plans to lower that to 3 percent in coming years. In finalizing its plan earlier this year, the Pennsylvania Public Utility Commission stated that eliminating cost recovery for gas lost above the cap shifts the financial burden of lost gas from the ratepayer to the gas company. That approach appears to have worked in Texas, which reduced its inventory of leak-prone service lines by an impressive 55 percent over the last two years. As noted earlier, the Massachusetts legislature is considering a cap on allowable unaccounted for gas. . . .

American consumers, businesses and communities now pay for gas they don't receive and bear the risks of gas leaks they cannot repair. Gas distribution companies, on the other hand, have little reason to treat leaky pipelines as an urgent problem. They may even make money off of lost gas because they're reimbursed whether it reaches the home or not. The Markey legislation will help make sure gas companies take responsibility and fix their leaks.

| "It doesn't look like there's way more
| failures happening."

Pipeline Safety Is Improving

Karl Henkel

Karl Henkel is a reporter for Vindy.com, a Youngstown, Ohio, news site. In the following viewpoint, he explains that gas explosions in Allentown, Pennsylvania, and San Bruno, California, have raised concerns about the safety of natural gas pipelines. He states that Ohio has taken several steps to prevent accidents and improve safety. Among these steps are audits of natural gas lines and replacement of aging pipelines. Despite the explosions, pipeline officials believe that safety is improving, he states.

As you read, consider the following questions:

1. What are some examples of steps that the Public Utilities Commission of Ohio takes when it detects a violation, according to Henkel?

2. According to the viewpoint, how are gas transmission lines checked?

3. According to the Pipeline and Hazardous Materials Safety Administration website, how many significant gas distribution incidents occurred in Ohio from 2001 to 2010, and what was the average across the United States?

About two weeks ago [February 9, 2011], residents of Allentown, Pa., became the latest victims of natural-gas leaks and explosions, when five died after an unexpected blast.

It was another highly documented blast, similar to one in San Bruno, Calif., which killed eight in September [2010].

Closer to home in Columbiana County on Feb. 10, a 36-inch pipe exploded in an open field. The explosion reportedly shook nearby homes but injured no one.

And that incident is on the heels of explosions in Fairport Harbor on Jan. 24 that destroyed 10 buildings and caused evacuation of more than 1,500 residents.

Ohio Takes Safety Measures

So how safe are Ohio's natural-gas pipelines, and could a deadly explosion happen in the Buckeye State?

Though various aspects—faulty computer systems and incorrect pipe sealing—have been blamed in other accidents, Ohio is trying to take steps to prevent natural-gas accidents and improve safety.

Each state is required to follow federal mandates from the Pipeline and Hazardous Materials Safety Administration. In Ohio the Public Utilities Commission of Ohio [PUCO], a state regulator of utility services, oversees natural-gas providers such as Columbia Gas of Ohio, Everflow Eastern, Inc. and Dominion East Ohio, according to Matt Butler, spokesman for the PUCO.

Butler said PUCO enforces all federally mandated natural-gas laws and said Ohio has nine investigators auditing every natural-gas line in the system at least once every two years.

He said the audits include spot and office-record checks and when PUCO detects a violation, it can assess fines and other penalties to help "minimize similar errors in the future."

PUCO can issue fines up to $100,000 per day for intrastate violations, Butler said. It's up to the federal government to assess fines on interstate pipelines, normally large distribution pipes.

In 2010, PUCO issued 29 "letters of probable non-compliance" to pipeline operators, which included 122 violations. In all 29 instances, the operator "remedied the violation[s] or submitted a plan for how they will address the violations," Butler said.

One of those last year dealt with Dominion East Ohio—operators of the nation's largest natural-gas storage system. Dominion could not document completion of some of its leak surveys in a "timely manner."

Butler said Dominion "agreed to perform a manual review of all 52,800 leak-survey areas, comparing leak-survey data from old leak-survey systems, their centralized compliance tracking database, and their GIS database" and "agreed to submit quarterly status reports to PUCO . . . beginning April 1, 2010."

Dominion also agreed to a $300,000 civil forfeiture if it didn't fulfill its obligations by Aug. 31. It followed through, and no fine was assessed.

John Williams, PUCO's director of service monitoring and enforcement, said Dominion couldn't properly document whether it had done the leak tests, so it was required to re-check them.

In the Jan. 24 explosion in Fairport Harbor, Dominion, in its preliminary report, could not determine why its pipes became over-pressurized. A follow-up report is due in late March.

Dave Rau, communications and community-relations manager at Columbia Gas Ohio, said his company had one reportable incident last year, when its Toledo facility caught fire in November. Though the final report is not yet completed, a third-party preliminary report said the "fire was caused by a power line that fell onto the facility," said Rau, who added the power line fell during a storm.

Columbia Gas of Ohio serves 61 of 88 Ohio counties—including Mahoning, Trumbull and Columbiana—and spans more than 25,000 square miles. Its customer base tops 1.4 million and is the largest natural-gas utility in the state.

In 2008, it began a 25-year, $2 billion project to replace aging pipes as preventive maintenance.

Steel and cast-iron distribution pipes will be replaced with much sturdier plastic that Rau hopes will "last for generations."

"It reaches a point where it becomes more expensive to fix a leak than it is to replace it [pipe]," he said.

Rau said transmission lines are inspected every seven years using one of three techniques: inline inspection, or "smart pigging," where a computer collects and records information about a pipeline, pressure testing and direct assessment, where instruments above ground excavate some of the pipeline for testing. In addition, leak surveys are done twice a year.

Distribution lines are tested more regularly. Pipes in business districts are tested every year, according to Columbia, every five years if the pipe is outside a business district and made of plastic or cathodically protected steel, every three years if it has a mixture of plastic or steel or all steel and is outside a business district.

Rau said streets or areas are not neglected based on their population.

"If there's a block or two that have just a few people, they'll be lumped into a larger area," he said.

The explosion in Columbiana County, which erupted on a farm, was a gas line operated by Tennessee Gas Pipeline Co.

Comparative Statistics for Petroleum Incident Rates: Onshore Transmission Pipelines vs. Road and Railway (2005–2009)

Mode	Avg. Billions Ton-Miles Shipment Per Year	Avg. Incidents Per Year	Incidents Per Billion Ton-Miles
Road*	34.8	695.2	19.95
Railway*	23.9	49.6	2.08
Hazardous Liquid Pipeline	584.1	339.6	0.58
Natural Gas Pipeline	338.5	299.2	0.89

*Only incidents involving and ton-mileage carrying those products carried by pipeline (petroleum products, liquid natural gas, etc.) are counted for road and railway.

TAKEN FROM: Diana Furchtgott-Roth, "Pipelines Are Safest for Transportation of Oil and Gas," Manhattan Institute for Policy Research, June 2013.

Pipeline Explosions Have Decreased

Richard Wheatley, a spokesman for Tennessee Gas, said the pipe was tested according to regulations, including leak surveys. The last documented leak survey on the pipeline in Columbiana County was in May 2010, and the company did visual and aerial checks in November. Wheatley also said an aerial check had occurred "several days" before the Feb. 10 accident.

Tennessee Gas is investigating the explosion.

Carl Weimer, executive director of Pipeline Safety Trust, a nonprofit public charity promoting fuel-transportation safety, said despite the highly visible recent cases in San Bruno, Allentown and Columbiana County, pipeline explosions have decreased.

"I think there's been kind of a heightened awareness," Weimer said. "There was the big oil spill in Michigan [when a pipeline spilled more than one million gallons of Canadian tar sand crude into the Kalamazoo River], then there was the San Bruno explosion and now Allentown. Those stories are making the media more, so everybody's more aware of pipelines and pipeline failures."

According to the PHMSA website, there were 32 significant gas distribution incidents in Ohio from 2001 to 2010, resulting in 16 injuries, four deaths and more than $10 million in damage.

The annual U.S. average is 76 incidents, 43 injuries and 11 deaths.

"When you look at the actual statistics, with the raw number of failures happening across the country, it hasn't really changed very much," Weimer said. "It doesn't look like there's way more failures happening."

> *"Each inspector is responsible for almost enough pipe to circle the earth."*

Pipeline Safety Chief Says Regulatory Process Is "Kind of Dying"

Marcus Stern and Sebastian Jones

Marcus Stern is a Pulitzer Prize–winning journalist and an investigative researcher for Strategic Research. Sebastian Jones is a reporter who has written for the Nation, Harper's, *and the* American Prospect. *In the following viewpoint, Stern and Jones reveal that Jeffrey Wiese, an official with the Department of Transportation's Pipeline and Hazardous Materials Safety Administration, admits that there are insufficient regulations in place to ensure the safety of natural gas pipelines. According to Wiese, the pipeline safety program is underfunded due to Congress's inability to pass a realistic budget. Only a fifth of the country's 2.6 million miles of pipeline has been inspected since 2006, the reporters explain.*

As you read, consider the following questions:

1. According to the viewpoint, how many federal inspectors oversee the nation's 2.6 million miles of pipeline?

2. What are some of the challenges facing pipeline regulators, according to the authors?

3. Why does Wiese think it takes too long to issue regulations?

Jeffrey Wiese, the nation's top oil and gas pipeline safety official, recently strode to a dais beneath crystal chandeliers at a New Orleans hotel to let his audience in on an open secret: the regulatory process he oversees is "kind of dying."

Wiese told several hundred oil and gas pipeline compliance officers that his agency, the Pipeline and Hazardous Materials Safety Administration (PHMSA), has "very few tools to work with" in enforcing safety rules even after Congress in 2011 allowed it to impose higher fines on companies that cause major accidents.

"Do I think I can hurt a major international corporation with a $2 million civil penalty? No," he said.

Because generating a new pipeline rule can take as long as three years, Wiese said PHMSA is creating a YouTube channel to persuade the industry to voluntarily improve its safety operations. "We'll be trying to socialize these concepts long before we get to regulations."

Wiese's pessimism about the viability of the pipeline regulatory system is at odds with the [Barack] Obama administration's insistence that the nation's pipeline infrastructure is safe and its regulatory regime robust. In a speech last year [2012], President Obama ordered regulatory agencies like PHMSA to help expedite the building of new pipelines "in a way that protects the health and safety of the American people."

Wiese's remarks also conflict with the industry's view. Brian Straessle, a spokesman for the American Petroleum Institute, which represents much of the oil and gas industry in Washington, D.C., said the industry "is highly regulated at the state and federal level, and there are strong standards in place to govern the pipeline infrastructure that helps fuel our economy."

"Pipeline operators have every incentive to protect the environment and their financial health by preventing incidents," Straessle said.

But Wiese's remarks ring true with people who've long been concerned about pipelines near their homes.

Susan Luebbe, a Nebraska rancher who has fought for five years to keep the proposed Keystone XL pipeline from crossing her cattle ranch, reacted with bemusement when Wiese's comments were relayed to her by cell phone as she repaired a barbed-wire fence. She and other Keystone opponents have long been suspicious of assurances by TransCanada, the company building the line, that it will be safe because it will meet or exceed PHMSA regulations.

"It's kind of sad in a way, when we push for laws to be enforced and they just throw up their hands, PHMSA and all of them, and say they can't deal with it," Luebbe said.

Public confidence in pipeline safety has been tested by a spate of serious accidents. In 2010, a natural gas line explosion in San Bruno, Calif., set off a 95-minute inferno that killed eight people, destroyed 38 homes and damaged scores of others. That same year, a pipeline spilled more than 1 million gallons of Canadian tar sand crude into Michigan's Kalamazoo River. The ongoing cleanup of that one spill has already cost more than $1 billion. This year, a pipeline rupture deposited at least 210,000 gallons of heavy Canadian crude in the streets of Mayflower, Ark.

Wiese, as head of PHMSA's Office of Pipeline Safety, is the federal official most directly charged with preventing these types of accidents. But as his July 24 comments in New Orleans reflect, he is constrained by a pipeline safety budget that has remained flat at about $108 million for the past three years, despite the construction of thousands of miles of new pipeline. Most of that money comes from industry user fees and an oil spill liability trust fund. Taxpayers pay just $1 million a year toward the safety program.

The Obama administration has consistently asked for more money for pipeline safety, but those requests have fallen victim to Congress's inability to pass anything more than stopgap budgets for the past three years. The administration asked for a 60 percent increase for this year, but the continuing budget standoff and effects of sequestration instead have tightened the budget.

Two stark numbers illustrate the challenge the administration faces in ensuring pipeline safety while pressing ahead with new pipeline projects: 135 federal inspectors oversee 2.6 million miles of pipeline, which means each inspector is responsible for almost enough pipe to circle the earth. PHMSA says it has the help of about 300 state inspectors, but not all states have inspection programs.

According to an analysis of inspection records by the non-profit Public Employees for Environmental Responsibility (PEER), only a fifth of the nation's 2.6 million miles of pipeline have been inspected by PHMSA or its state partners since 2006. PEER obtained the records through the Freedom of Information Act.

InsideClimate News tried for several weeks to arrange an interview with Wiese about his remarks. At one point PHMSA spokesman Damon Hill wrote in an e-mail, "I'm trying to help you get what you need for your story and in no way are we saying that Mr. Wiese or anyone else in PHMSA is unavailable to provide information or clarifications."

But Hill didn't respond to subsequent e-mails requesting to speak with Wiese and other PHMSA staffers who attended the pipeline safety conference in New Orleans, and Wiese didn't respond to interview requests sent to his official e-mail address.

PHMSA: A Thin Green Line Protecting the Public from Spills and Explosions

PHMSA was created in 2004 as an agency within the federal Department of Transportation. It is a thin green line intended to ensure the safety of energy pipelines that crisscross the United States. Pipelines also carry other hazardous materials, including poisonous, carcinogenic chemicals like benzene. The agency's tasks include auditing the records of almost 3,000 pipeline operators; developing, issuing and enforcing pipeline safety regulations; conducting industry training, and investigating accidents.

The challenges facing regulators are daunting. More than half of the nation's pipeline was buried prior to 1970, about the same time the nation's first pipeline safety law was enacted and the Office of Pipeline Safety created. Much of the old pipe remains a question mark in terms of its location, composition, level of corrosion and quality of welding.

Some pipelines in the East are more than 100 years old. In the West, suburbs have grown up alongside lines installed when the areas were uninhabited. Age is not necessarily a critical factor if pipe is properly installed, maintained and operated. But many pipelines have changed ownership so many times that installation and maintenance records are unavailable.

In its budget proposal for this year, PHMSA defended its record, stating that its work "often goes unnoticed due to its successful efforts in reducing and containing serious incidents." The agency included a chart showing that incidents resulting in death or serious injury declined more than 60 percent during that period even as the number of miles of pipeline increased almost 40 percent. Other PHMSA data show modest declines in the number of serious incidents, injuries and fatalities in recent years.

"PHMSA is moving in the right direction," said Ravindra Chhatre, an investigator at the National Transportation Safety

Board who specializes in pipeline accidents. "Sometimes people get frustrated by the pace that it's moving, but definitely it's improving."

Congress Delays Action on Shutoff Valves Even After Inferno Kills Eight

The problem, Wiese said in New Orleans, is that it takes too long to issue regulations, in part because the industry negotiates for the weakest possible rules.

"Getting any change through regulation, which used to be a viable tool, is no longer viable," Wiese told the industry representatives. "I really don't see that as a way to get change. It moves so slow. I've been working on rules now for recommendations from our friends at (the National Transportation Safety Board) and U.S. Congress. I've been working very hard but with the resources we have I still can't get those rules out."

To Rep. Jackie Speier, D-Calif., whose district includes the site of one the deadliest pipeline accidents in American history, Wiese's comments were surprising only because they were delivered in public.

"To me, he was refreshingly candid," she said. "The industry has a lock on PHMSA. It has a lock on Congress. And the public's interest gets dramatically watered down."

Speier began having doubts about PHMSA after a 30-inch section of pipe ruptured in San Bruno at 6:11 p.m. on Sept. 9, 2010. The explosion generated a giant fireball that went on for 95 minutes because it took that long for gas line operator Pacific Gas and Electric [PG&E] to reach the manual shutoff valves.

The pipe had been installed in 1956 and was substandard and poorly welded, a National Transportation Safety Board (NTSB) investigation found later. Because it was grandfathered under PHMSA's safety laws, it wasn't subjected to the pressure testing that newer pipes must undergo.

The NTSB's investigation also found widespread failures of PG&E's operations, maintenance, record-keeping systems and emergency response. It issued a total of 39 recommendations, including 13 to PHMSA. As the third anniversary of the explosion approaches, PHMSA has yet to finish implementing any of the recommendations, according to the NTSB.

One of those recommendations was for remote shutoff valves to be installed on energy pipelines near suburbs, dams or other areas where an explosion would have grave consequences. Safety advocates had been arguing for remote or automatic safety valves since the 1970s, but the oil and gas industry always objected, saying the cost was too high and false alarms could shut down a pipeline, disrupting the flow of oil or gas.

On the first anniversary of the tragedy that rocked her district, Speier introduced legislation designed to implement many of the NTSB recommendations, including the call for remote shutoff valves.

But the law President Obama signed several weeks later was a compromise bill—the Pipeline Safety, Regulatory Certainty, and Job Creation Act of 2011. It was praised in its final form by the American Petroleum Institute, the Interstate Natural Gas Association of America and other industry groups. It was far weaker than Speier's legislation, especially when it came to the remote shutoff valves that might have reduced the death and destruction in San Bruno.

Instead of requiring operators to install the valves quickly, the act directs PHMSA to spend a year studying the mechanics and costs of such a rule and then spend another year deliberating the implications. It also stipulates that PHMSA may not proceed down the road toward regulations—a process that typically takes 18 months to three years—until it first determines that remote shutoff valves are economically feasible for the industry. Even then, the new rule could be applied only to pipelines laid in the future.

Pipelines Are Often in Dangerous Locations

Companies have wide latitude in choosing where they put their pipelines. . . .

They often put pipelines near existing roads or pipelines, which may be in heavily populated areas, because those rights are easiest to purchase. . . .

Combined with what critics say is a lack of inspections on pipelines, the fact that pipelines are too close to people or rivers or other sensitive environments makes accidents, when they happen, more deadly and destructive.

Tina Lam, "Many Live Next to Dangerous Pipelines in Michigan," Detroit Free Press, *September 27, 2010.*

"Laughable," Speier said of the provision in a recent interview. Industry, which has argued for decades that remote shutoff valves are too costly, will no doubt continue to do so, she said.

Non-Industry Groups Find PHMSA Less Accessible

In addition to Wiese, PHMSA sent at least three officials to address the safety conference at the Royal Sonesta Hotel in New Orleans. Two former PHMSA officials who left the agency to work as industry consultants also addressed the group of 300 to 400 oil and gas pipeline operators. Throughout the week, the Louisiana Gas Association operated a hospitality suite overlooking Bourbon Street, where regulators and industry representatives gathered each evening to sip libations and drop beads to passersby.

Speaking just before Wiese, Bob Kipp, president of the Common Ground Alliance, an industry-backed safety group, drew on Sun Tzu's classic treatise, *The Art of War*, in urging the crowd to "keep your friends close and your regulators closer." The comment drew chuckles from the audience.

Groups outside the industry have found PHMSA far less accessible.

In preparing for a recent trip to Washington, a delegation organized by the National Wildlife Federation tried to set up appointments with the State Department, the Environmental Protection Agency [EPA] and PHMSA to discuss pipeline safety. While the delegation was welcomed by the State Department and the EPA, a PHMSA official denied the request without explanation.

To Beth Wallace, the federation's community outreach coordinator for the Great Lakes Regional Center, it was typical of the brush-offs environmental groups get from PHMSA. "It seems that the agency always gives an ear to the industry," she said. "But when it comes to public participation, there doesn't seem to be that same level of access."

PHMSA spokesman Hill said agency officials had met with the National Wildlife Federation in May and didn't feel another meeting was necessary.

In New Orleans, Wiese said "an under-informed populace highly dependent on fossil fuels" is prone to negative perceptions of the industry. He said that penchant is exacerbated by a press corps that doesn't "have time to fully understand the story" and has instead served as a vehicle for "gang warfare" through its coverage of events like the March 29th rupture of ExxonMobil's Pegasus pipeline in Mayflower, Ark.

Congress, Wiese contended, hasn't done much to help.

"It's very political in Washington. Nobody wants to try to figure out what's the best thing to do. They're thinking about what's the most advantageous position to take," he said, later adding that he'd recently had an unpleasant meeting with a "very hot" congressional delegation about the Pegasus spill in Arkansas.

Rep. Tim Griffin, R-Ark., a member of the delegation Wiese was referring to, has criticized the operations and maintenance of the pipeline and PHMSA's lack of transparency.

"If public officials and Arkansans would have known then what we know now, changes to the operation of the pipeline may have been demanded years ago," he said.

> *"Pipelines are generally regarded as a safe way to transport fuel, a far better alternative to tanker trucks or freight trains."*

Pipelines Explained: How Safe Are America's 2.5 Million Miles of Pipelines?

Lena Groeger

Lena Groeger is a writer for ProPublica. In the following viewpoint, she explains that although transporting oil and gas by pipelines is much safer than by train or truck transportation, critics believe pipeline transport should be even safer. The major problem is age, she reports, with more than half of the nation's pipelines at least fifty years old. Contributing to the problem is a lack of regulation and a lack of resources to inspect pipelines, Groeger adds.

As you read, consider the following questions:

1. According to the statistics the author quotes, how does pipeline safety compare with truck safety?

2. What are some of the reasons cited for pipeline break-age?

3. What does the author cite as the reason for lax oversight of pipelines?

At 6:11 p.m. on September 6, 2010, San Bruno, Calif., 911 received an urgent call. A gas station had just exploded and a fire with flames reaching 300 feet was raging through the neighborhood. The explosion was so large that residents suspected an airplane crash. But the real culprit was found underground: a ruptured pipeline spewing natural gas caused a blast that left behind a 72-foot-long crater, killed eight people, and injured more than fifty.

Over 2,000 miles away in Michigan, workers were still cleaning up another pipeline accident, which spilled 840,000 gallons of crude oil into the Kalamazoo River in 2010. Estimated to cost $800 million, the accident is the most expensive pipeline spill in U.S. history.

Over the last few years, a series of incidents have brought pipeline safety to national—and presidential—attention. As Obama begins his second term he will likely make a key decision on the controversial Keystone XL pipeline [1], a proposed pipeline extension to transport crude from Canada to the Gulf of Mexico.

The administration first delayed the permit for the pipeline on environmental grounds [2], but has left the door open to future proposals for Keystone's northern route. Construction on the southern route is already under way [3], sparking fierce opposition [4] from some landowners and environmentalists.

The problem, protesters say, is that any route will pose hazards to the public. While pipeline operator TransCanada has declared that Keystone will be the safest pipeline ever built [5] in North America, critics are skeptical.

"It's inevitable that as pipelines age, as they are exposed to the elements, eventually they are going to spill," said Tony Iallonardo of the National Wildlife Federation [6]. "They're ticking time bombs."

Critics of the Keystone proposal point to the hundreds of pipeline accidents that occur every year. They charge that system-wide, antiquated pipes, minimal oversight and inadequate precautions put the public and the environment at increasing risk. Pipeline operators point to billions of dollars spent on new technologies and a gradual improvement over the last two decades as proof of their commitment to safety.

Pipelines are generally regarded as a safe way to transport fuel, a far better alternative to tanker trucks or freight trains. The risks inherent in transporting fuel through pipelines are analogous in the risks inherent in traveling by airplane. Airplanes are safer than cars, which kill about 70 times as many people a year (highway accidents killed about 33,000 people in 2010 [7], while aviation accidents killed 472). But when an airplane crashes, it is much more deadly than any single car accident, demands much more attention, and initiates large investigations to determine precisely what went wrong.

The same holds true for pipelines. Based on fatality statistics from 2005 through 2009 [8], oil pipelines are roughly 70 times as safe as trucks, which killed four times as many people during those years, despite transporting only a tiny fraction of fuel shipments. But when a pipeline does fail, the consequences can be catastrophic (though typically less so than airplane accidents), with the very deadliest accidents garnering media attention and sometimes leading to a federal investigation.

While both air travel and pipelines are safer than their road alternatives, the analogy only extends so far. Airplanes are replaced routinely and older equipment is monitored regularly for airworthiness and replaced when it reaches its safety limits. Pipelines, on the other hand, can stay underground, carrying highly pressurized gas and oil for decades—even up to a century and beyond. And while airplanes have strict and uniform regulations and safety protocols put forth by the Federal Aviation Administration, such a uniform set of standards does not exist for pipelines.

Critics maintain that while they're relatively safe, pipelines should be safer. In many cases, critics argue, pipeline accidents could have been prevented with proper regulation from the government and increased safety measures by the industry. The 2.5 million miles of America's pipelines suffer hundreds of leaks and ruptures every year, costing lives and money. As existing lines grow older, critics warn that the risk of accidents on those lines will only increase.

While states with the most pipeline mileage—like Texas, California, and Louisiana—also have the most incidents, breaks occur throughout the far-flung network of pipelines. Winding under city streets and countryside, these lines stay invisible most of the time. Until they fail.

Since 1986, pipeline accidents have killed more than 500 people, injured over 4,000, and cost nearly seven billion dollars in property damages. Using government data, ProPublica has mapped thousands of these incidents in a new interactive news application [9], which provides detailed information about the cause and costs of reported incidents going back nearly three decades.

Pipelines break for many reasons—from the slow deterioration of corrosion to equipment or weld failures to construction workers hitting pipes [10] with their excavation equipment. Unforeseen natural disasters also lead to dozens of incidents a year. This year Hurricane Sandy wreaked havoc [11] on the natural gas pipelines on New Jersey's barrier islands. From Bay Head to Long Beach Island, falling trees, dislodged homes and flooding caused more than 1,600 pipeline leaks. All leaks have been brought under control [12] and no one was harmed, according to a New Jersey Natural Gas spokeswoman. But the company was forced to shut down service to the region, leaving 28,000 people without gas, and it may be months before they get it back.

One of the biggest problems contributing to leaks and ruptures is pretty simple: Pipelines are getting older. More than half of the nation's pipelines are at least 50 years old [13]. Last year in Allentown, Pa., a natural gas pipeline exploded underneath a city street, killing five people who lived in the houses above and igniting a fire that damaged 50 buildings. The pipeline—made of cast iron—had been installed in 1928.

Not all old pipelines are doomed to fail, but time is a big contributor to corrosion, a leading cause of pipeline failure. Corrosion has caused between 15 and 20 percent of all reported "significant incidents" [14], which is bureaucratic parlance for an incident that resulted in a death, injury or extensive property damage. That's over 1,400 incidents since 1986.

Corrosion is also cited as a chief concern of opponents of the Keystone XL extension. The new pipeline would transport a type of crude called diluted bitumen [15], or "dilbit." Keystone's critics make the case [16] that the chemical makeup of this heavier type of oil is much more corrosive than conventional oil, and over time could weaken the pipeline.

Operator TransCanada says that the Keystone XL pipeline will transport crude similar [15] to what's been piped into the U.S. for more than a decade, and that the new section of pipeline will be built and tested to meet all federal safety requirements. And in fact, none of the 14 spills that happened in the existing keystone pipeline since 2010 were caused by corrosion, according to an investigation by the U.S. Department of State [17].

The specific effects of dilbit on pipelines—and whether the heavy crude would actually lead to more accidents—is not definitively understood by scientists. The National Academy of Sciences is currently in the middle of study on dilbit and pipeline corrosion [18], due out by next year. In the meantime, TransCanada has already begun construction of the southern portion of the line, but has no assurance it will get a permit from the Obama administration to build the northern section. (NPR has a detailed map of the existing and proposed routes [1].)

Little Government Regulation for Thousands of Miles

While a slew of federal and state agencies oversee some aspect of America's pipelines, the bulk of government monitoring and enforcement falls to a small agency within the Department of Transportation called the Pipeline and Hazardous Materials Safety Administration—[19] pronounced "FIM-sa" by insiders. The agency only requires that seven percent of natural gas lines and 44 percent of all hazardous liquid lines be subject to their rigorous inspection criteria and inspected regularly. The rest of the regulated pipelines are still inspected, according to a PHMSA official, but less often.

The inconsistent rules and inspection regime come in part from a historical accident. In the 60s and 70s, two laws established a federal role in pipeline safety [20] and set national rules for new pipelines. For example, operators were required to conduct more stringent testing to see whether pipes could withstand high pressures, and had to meet new specifications for how deep underground pipelines must be installed.

But the then-new rules mostly didn't apply to pipelines already built—such as the pipeline that exploded in San Bruno. That pipeline, which burst open along a defective seam weld, would never have passed modern high-pressure requirements according to a federal investigation [21]. But because it was installed in 1956, it was never required to.

"No one wanted all the companies to dig up and retest their pipelines," explained Carl Weimer, executive director of the Pipeline Safety Trust [22], a public charity that promotes fuel transportation safety. So older pipes were essentially grandfathered into less testing, he said.

Later reforms in the 1990s mandated more testing for oil pipelines, and today PHMSA requires operators to test pipelines in "high consequence" areas, which include population centers or areas near drinking water. But many old pipelines in rural areas aren't covered by the same strict regulations.

Some types of pipelines—such as the "gathering" lines that connect wells to process facilities or larger transmission lines—lack any PHMSA regulation at all. A GAO report [23] estimates that of the roughly 230,000 miles of gathering lines, only 24,000 are federally regulated. Because many of these lines operate at lower pressures and generally go through remote areas, says the GAO, the government collects no data on ruptures or spills, and has no enforced standards for pipeline strength, welds, or underground depth on the vast majority of these pipes.

The problem, critics argue [24], is that today's gathering lines no longer match their old description. Driven in part by the rising demands of hydraulic fracturing, operators have built thousands of miles of new lines to transport gas from fracked wells. Despite the fact that these lines are often just as wide as transmission lines (some up to 2 feet in diameter) and can operate under the same high pressures, they receive little oversight.

Operators use a risk-based system to maintain their pipelines—instead of treating all pipelines equally, they focus safety efforts on the lines deemed most risky, and those that would cause the most harm if they failed. The problem is that each company use different criteria, so "it's a nightmare for regulators," Weimer said.

However, Andrew Black, the president of the Association of Oil Pipe Lines, a trade group whose members include pipeline operators, said that a one-size-fits-all approach would actually make pipelines less safe, because operators (not to mention pipelines) differ so widely.

"Different operators use different pipe components, using different construction techniques, carrying different materials over different terrains," he said. Allowing operators to develop their own strategies for each pipeline is critical to properly maintaining its safety, he contended.

Limited Resources Leave Inspections to Industry

Critics say that PHMSA lacks the resources to adequately monitor [25] the millions of miles of pipelines over which it *does* have authority. The agency has funding for only 137 inspectors, and often employs even less than that (in 2010 the agency had 110 inspectors on staff). A Congressional Research Service report [26] found a "long-term pattern of understaffing" in the agency's pipeline safety program. According to the report, between 2001 and 2009 the agency reported a staffing shortfall of an average of 24 employees a year.

A *New York Times* investigation last year found that the agency is chronically short of inspectors because it just doesn't have enough money to hire more [27], possibly due to competition from the pipeline companies themselves, who often hire away PHMSA inspectors for their corporate safety programs, according to the CRS.

Given the limitations of government money and personnel, it is often the industry that inspects its own pipelines. Although federal and state inspectors review paperwork and conduct audits, most on-site pipeline inspections are done by inspectors on the company's dime.

The industry's relationship with PHMSA may go further than inspections, critics say. The agency has adopted, at least in part, dozens of safety standards written by the oil and natural gas industry.[28]

"This isn't like the fox guarding the hen house," said Weimer. "It's like the fox designing the hen house."

Operators point out that defining their own standards allows the inspection system to tap into real-world expertise. Adopted standards go through a rulemaking process that gives stakeholders and the public a chance to comment and suggest changes, according to the agency.

Questions have also been raised about the ties between agency officials and the companies they regulate [29]. Before joining the agency in 2009, PHMSA administrator Cynthia Quarterman worked as a legal counsel for Enbridge Energy, the operator involved in the Kalamazoo River accident. But under her leadership, the agency has also brought a record number of enforcement cases against operators [30], and imposed the highest civil penalty in the agency's history [31] on the company she once represented.

Proposed Solutions Spark Debate

How to adequately maintain the diversity of pipelines has proved to be a divisive issue—critics arguing for more automatic tests and safety measures and companies pointing to the high cost of such additions.

One such measure is the widespread installation of automatic or remote-controlled shutoff valves, which can quickly stop the flow of gas or oil in an emergency. These valves could help avoid a situation like that after the Kalamazoo River spill, which took operators 17 hours from the initial rupture to find and manually shut off. Operators use these valves already on most new pipelines, but argue that replacing all valves would not be cost-effective and false alarms would unnecessarily shut down fuel supplies. The CRS estimates that even if automatic valves were only required on pipelines in highly populated areas, replacing manual valves with automatic ones could cost the industry hundreds of millions of dollars.

Other measures focus on preventing leaks and ruptures in the first place. The industry already uses robotic devices called "smart pigs" [32] to crawl through a pipeline, clearing debris and taking measurements to detect any problems [33]. But not all pipelines can accommodate smart pigs, and operators don't routinely run the devices through every line.

Just last month, a smart pig detected a "small anomaly" in the existing Keystone pipeline, prompting TransCanada to shut down the entire line. Environmentalists pointed out that this is not the first time TransCananda has called for a shut down, and won't be the last.

"The reason TransCanada needs to keep shutting down Keystone," the director of the National Wildlife Federation contended in a statement [34], "is because pipelines are inherently dangerous."

Last January, Obama signed a bill [35] that commissioned several new studies [36] to evaluate some of these proposed safety measures, although his decision on extending the Keystone pipeline may come long before those studies are completed.

Notes

1. http://stateimpact.npr.org/texas/tag/keystone-xl-pipeline/

2. http://www.whitehouse.gov/the-press-office/2011/11/10/statement-president
-state-departments-keystone-xl-pipeline-announcement

3. http://articles.latimes.com/2012/aug/16/nation/la-na-nn-keystone-xl-pipeline
-20120816

4. http://www.nytimes.com/2012/10/13/us/protesters-gather-at-keystone-xl-site-in
-texas.html?_r=0

5. http://www.transcanada.com/6059.html

6. http://www.nwf.org/

7. http://www.ntsb.gov/data/index.html

8. http://www.manhattan-institute.org/html/ib_23.htm#.VA2i42Na_5Q

9. http://projects.propublica.org/pipelines/

10. http://www.call811.com/

11. http://articles.philly.com/2012-11-05/news/34931014_1_natural-gas-gas-line-seaside-heights

12. http://www.njng.com/safety/hurricane-sandy-updates/index.asp

13. http://opsweb.phmsa.dot.gov/pipelineforum/docs/Secretarys%20Infrastructure%20Report_Revised%20per%20PHC_103111.pdf

14. http://primis.phmsa.dot.gov/comm/reports/safety/sigpsi.html

15. http://insideclimatenews.org/news/20120626/dilbit-primer-diluted-bitumen-conventional-oil-tar-sands-Alberta-Kalamazoo-Keystone-XL-Enbridge

16. http://www.nrdc.org/energy/tarsandssafetyrisks.asp

17. http://keystonepipeline-xl.state.gov/documents/organization/181185.pdf

18. http://www8.nationalacademies.org/cp/projectview.aspx?key=49461

19. http://www.phmsa.dot.gov/

20. http://phmsa.dot.gov/pipeline/state-programs

21. http://www.ntsb.gov/doclib/reports/2011/PAR1101.pdf

22. http://pstrust.org/

23. http://www.gao.gov/products/GAO-12-388

24. http://switchboard.nrdc.org/blogs/amall/many_hazards_from_natural_gas.html

25. http://www.philly.com/philly/news/special_packages/inquirer/marcellus-shale/20111210_Federal_pipeline_oversight_agency_was_troubled_from_the_start.html

26. http://fas.org/sgp/crs/homesec/R41536.pdf

27. http://www.nytimes.com/2011/09/10/business/energy-environment/agency-struggles-to-safeguard-pipeline-system.html?ref=danfrosch&_r=0

28. http://washingtonindependent.com/94743/oil-and-gas-industry-writes-its-own-pipeline-standards

29. http://www.nytimes.com/gwire/2010/09/17/17greenwire-critics-fault-oil-and-gas-pipeline-regulators-i-9153.html

30. http://phmsa.dot.gov/pv_obj_cache/pv_obj_id_7B23A0E4393E956BD34C44F9A7953BD38FB40000/filename/Record%20Enforcement%20Orders%20Closed_02-08-12.pdf

31. http://www.freep.com/article/20120911/NEWS05/309110050/Enbridge-pays-3-7M-penalty-in-10-oil-spill

32. http://www.buckeye.com/pipelineawareness/keepingyousafepipelinesecurity/smartpigs/tabid/106/default.aspx

33. http://www.npr.org/templates/story/story.php?storyId=5627707

Natural Gas

34. http://blog.nwf.org/2012/10/original-keystone-pipeline-shuts-down-safety-a
-concern/

35. http://www.propublica.org/article/congress-moves-toward-tougher-stand-on
-pipeline-safety-but-is-it-enough

36. http://www.gpo.gov/fdsys/pkg/BILLS-112hconres93enr/pdf/BILL-
112hconres93enr.pdf

Periodical and Internet Sources Bibliography

The following articles have been selected to supplement the diverse views presented in this chapter.

Jeff Brady	"After Deaths, Renewed Focus on Leaky Gas Pipelines," *NPR*, April 14, 2014.
Concord Monitor (New Hampshire)	"Editorial: Wanted: New Natural Gas Pipelines," January 30, 2014.
Energy & Commerce Committee, US House of Representatives	"Consumers Desperate for New Natural Gas Pipelines," February 5, 2014.
Environment News Service	"TransCanada Natural Gas Pipeline Explodes in Manitoba," January 27, 2014.
Clifford Krauss and Eric Lipton	"After the Boom in Natural Gas," *New York Times*, October 20, 2012.
Leonard Lance	"Opinion: More Natural Gas Pipelines in U.S. Would Result in Lower Energy Costs," NJ.com, January 25, 2014.
Amy Joi O'Donoghue	"Natural Gas Pipeline Is a Line in the Sand," *Deseret News* (Salt Lake City, UT), April 12, 2014.
Dallas Parker, John D. Furlow, and Mayer Brown	"Need for Infrastructure Among Challenges Outside of U.S.: Prospects of a Global Shale Revolution, Part 2," *Pipeline & Gas Journal*, November 2013.
Matthew Philips	"Northeast's Record Natural Gas Prices Due to Pipeline Dearth," *Bloomberg Businessweek*, February 6, 2014.
James West	"Charts: How Dangerous Are the Gas Pipelines Under Your City?," *Mother Jones*, March 21, 2014.

OPPOSING
VIEWPOINTS®
SERIES

CHAPTER 3

Should the United States Export Natural Gas?

Chapter Preface

A s the United States and Russia faced off in early 2014 over Russia's campaign to restore the Crimean peninsula to Russian control, both sides had the potential to use natural gas as an unconventional weapon. Both Russia and the United States have vast supplies of natural gas; the Ukraine, like much of Europe, has few gas fields. Europe gets approximately one-third of its natural gas from Russia, with 40 percent of it running through pipelines traversing the Ukraine.

Russia cut off gas supplies to the Ukraine in both 2006 and 2009, and it threatened to do so again in 2014. In April 2014, Russian president Vladimir Putin threatened to restrict supplies of natural gas to the Ukraine, contending that the Ukraine owed Russia more than $16 billion in unpaid gas bills and other debts. According to David M. Herszenhorn in an April 9, 2014, article in the *New York Times*, "[These threats] were the latest pointed reminders to the West that Russia holds substantial sway over Ukraine's financial future—even without a military incursion into eastern Ukraine. The declarations also seemed intended to increase the Kremlin's leverage in talks with the United States over resolving the political crisis."

However, some commentators argue that Putin's move was short-sighted, as its effect would force Europe to wean itself from its reliance on Russian natural gas. Following Russia's cutoff of gas supplies to Europe in 2006 and 2009, imports from Norway and Qatar were increased, and new facilities for storing liquefied natural gas were built. In the wake of the Crimean crisis, British foreign secretary William Hague said the crisis was likely to make Europe "recast" its approach to energy. According to James Surowiecki in a March 24, 2014, article in the *New Yorker*, "Alienating customers and giving competitors an opening isn't just bad business. It's bad politics. Putin likes to think of himself as a geopolitical grandmaster. But when it comes to natural gas he isn't thinking enough moves ahead."

Opinion is also divided on whether the United States should begin exporting gas to Europe in response to Russian threats to cut off gas to the Ukraine. According to Chip Register, managing director of Sapient Global Markets, "The U.S. could supply 10% to 20% of Europe's natural gas needs by 2015 and over a quarter by 2020. . . . When combined with increased exports from Nigeria and the Middle East, as well as their own fracking initiatives, Europe could potentially be off Russian gas in just a few short years."

However, others, including Sierra Club senior director Athan Manuel, say exporting gas to Europe is impractical, because the United States does not have the physical capacity to export liquefied natural gas. According to Daniel Dicker, oil trader and CNBC contributor, even if construction of exporting facilities were expedited "there may be an even more important question to ask: Should our nation open up our own limited natural gas resources to be used as a stopgap for European energy dependence on Russia? Is the U.S. ready to become a fracking mecca supplying the rest of the West with energy, while they happily shun traditional energy development and pursue renewables?"

Along with geopolitical issues, there are also environmental and economic controversies surrounding the question of exporting natural gas. Scientists, commentators, and journalists explore these issues in the following chapter.

| "Enlightened leadership and a strategy that mitigates downsides for poorer consumers and the local environment are essential to a smart strategy for constructively moving exports forward."

The Benefits of Exporting Natural Gas Are Greater than the Risks

Michael Levi

Michael Levi is the David M. Rubenstein Senior Fellow for Energy and the Environment at the Council on Foreign Relations and director of the council's program on geoeconomic studies. He is the author of On Nuclear Terrorism. *In the following viewpoint, Levi states that the use of fracking has significantly increased the supply of natural gas in the United States and has resulted in lower gas prices. Benchmark gas prices in early 2012 were more than five times lower in the United States than in Europe and more than seven times lower than in Asia, causing many to press lawmakers to allow the exporting of natural gas, he reports. Levi concludes that the benefits of allowing exports outweigh the potential downside risks, as long as appropriate environmental protections are in place.*

As you read, consider the following questions:

1. According to the author, what are the concerns of those who oppose exporting natural gas?

2. What six factors does the author urge policy makers to weigh in making a decision concerning exporting natural gas?

3. What benefits does the author see to the exporting of natural gas?

U.S. natural gas production is booming. Five years ago [in 2007], most experts assumed that U.S. natural gas output was in terminal decline; today, most believe the opposite. As recently as 2009, the U.S. Department of Energy was projecting indefinite dependence on imported natural gas along with rising prices for decades to come. By 2010, after breakthroughs in extracting natural gas from shale, conventional wisdom had flipped. Large-scale gas imports now seem unlikely, and abundant domestic supplies look like they will hold prices in check.

Gas in the United States Is Comparatively Cheap

The market has signaled its endorsement of this development by hammering natural gas prices. U.S. benchmark natural gas dipped below $2 for a thousand cubic feet in early 2012, and as of mid-April 2012, delivery of the same amount in March 2015 could be assured for $4.43. Wellhead prices, meanwhile, fell to levels unseen since 1995.

But the world looks different from overseas. In Europe, a thousand cubic feet of gas sold on the spot market for about $11 as of March 2012, and in East Asia, the price was north of $15. These prices are all the more striking since it costs roughly $4 to liquefy and ship a thousand cubic feet of natural gas from the United States to Europe, and only about $2 more to send it to Asia.

Yet the United States does not export natural gas to those markets. Many have thus argued that it is leaving money on the table. The potential profits from exports have prompted several companies to apply for permits to export liquefied natural gas (LNG) without restriction. In March 2011, the U.S. Department of Energy (DOE) approved the first such permit, for Cheniere Energy, and in April 2012, the Federal Energy Regulatory Commission (FERC) approved Cheniere's Sabine Pass, Louisiana facility. As of May 2012, another eight projects had applied to the DOE for similar permits, and four more had applied for permits to export LNG to countries with which the United States has free trade agreements. The DOE has signaled that it will begin making decisions on these applications after receiving the results of a contractor study on the possible impacts of LNG exports. . . . The DOE can be expected to solicit input from several agencies, including the Departments of State and Commerce, the Environmental Protection Agency, and the Office of the U.S. Trade Representative, as well as from the National Economic Council, the National Security Council, and the Council on Environmental Quality in making its ultimate decisions.

Indeed, if currently anticipated price differences hold up, and fully free trade in natural gas is allowed, several developers will likely attempt to build LNG export terminals. A wide range of analysts have claimed that as many as six billion cubic feet of daily exports by the end of the decade is plausible. That trade could expand U.S. gas production substantially and, in principle, net U.S. producers, exporters, and their suppliers north of $10 billion a year. Gas exports could help narrow the U.S. current account deficit, shake up geopolitics, and give the United States new leverage in trade negotiations. This has led many people to advocate for a U.S. policy that allows—or even encourages—natural gas exports.

There Are Concerns Regarding Exporting Gas

But there is also great wariness in many quarters about the prospect of allowing exports of natural gas. Americans usually support exports, but natural gas, along with other energy commodities, has recently received special scrutiny. Some fear that allowing exports would dangerously drive up domestic natural gas prices while making the U.S. gas market more volatile. Others would prefer that domestic gas be directed toward boosting manufacturing at home, replacing coal-fired power plants, or taking the place of oil as the ultimate fuel for American cars and trucks. Still more oppose natural gas exports because those exports would result in greater U.S. natural gas production, potentially leading to social and environmental disruption. All of these parties oppose natural gas exports, or at least seek significant constraints. Some are driven by broad visions of the national interest to conclude that natural gas exports would have negative consequences that are not captured by simple economic logic. Others are motivated by more self-interested concerns, particularly the desire to secure cheap energy inputs for their industries.

There is also skepticism in some quarters over whether LNG exports, even if allowed, will ever get off the ground. Yet with a large docket of export applications pending, policy makers will have no choice but to step into this controversy. In this [viewpoint], I elaborate a framework for policy makers to use in deciding whether to allow LNG exports (a decision for regulators) or whether to take steps to constrain them (a decision for both regulators and lawmakers). This framework should focus on evaluating six questions:

1. What broad economic gains and losses might allowing LNG exports deliver?

2. How might exports affect energy bills for people of limited economic means?

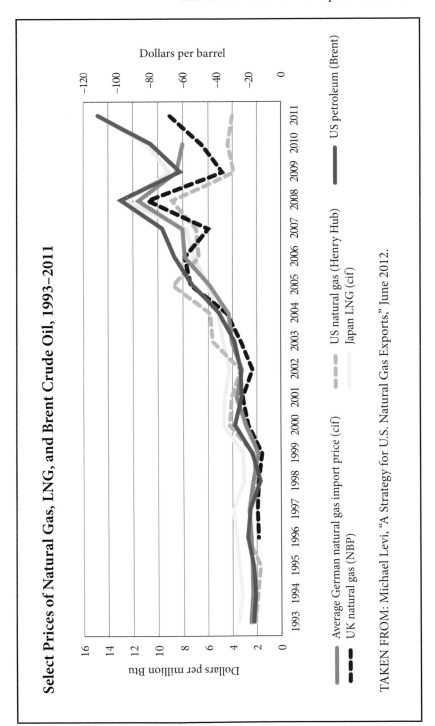

Select Prices of Natural Gas, LNG, and Brent Crude Oil, 1993–2011

Dollars per barrel

Dollars per million Btu

US petroleum (Brent)

US natural gas (Henry Hub)
Japan LNG (cif)

Average German natural gas import price (cif)
UK natural gas (NBP)

TAKEN FROM: Michael Levi, "A Strategy for U.S. Natural Gas Exports," June 2012.

3. Would LNG exports undermine U.S. energy security by preventing the United States from using more natural gas in its cars and trucks?

4. Would exports help or hurt the fight against climate change?

5. How would different U.S. decisions on exports affect U.S. foreign policy, including broad U.S. access to global markets in particular?

6. Would allowing exports lead to more U.S. natural gas production—and if production increases, what would the consequences be for the local environment?

This [viewpoint] addresses these questions and argues that the benefits from allowing natural gas exports outweigh the commonly cited risks and costs, assuming that proper steps are taken to protect the environment.

Gas Exports Have Economic and Political Benefits

The potential direct economic gains from LNG exports are significant but they are also smaller than many assume. Export terminal construction might employ as many as 8,000 people at different points over the next several years, but these jobs will be temporary. Expanding natural gas production in order to supply export markets could potentially support roughly 25,000 jobs in the natural gas industry, and perhaps 40,000 along the supply chain, but most of these positions would not materialize for at least five more years, and can thus be reasonably expected to be mostly offset by lower employment elsewhere. Profits from greater gas production and export activities could reach several billion dollars each year, while losses to other gas dependent industries would likely be at least an order of magnitude smaller. Indeed, the resurgent petrochemicals industry, which many have assumed would suffer from gas exports, would be more likely to benefit instead from modest export volumes.

Moreover, allowing LNG exports would have benefits for U.S. leverage in trade diplomacy, potentially delivering wider economic benefits. Conversely, placing curbs on U.S. LNG exports could undermine U.S. access to exports from other markets (including to Chinese rare earth metals, which are essential to many segments of the U.S. clean energy industry), and could potentially result in broader trade conflicts, leading to wider U.S. economic harm.

To be certain, changes in world gas markets could reduce opportunities for LNG exports, and thus any benefits from allowing them. But that would not change the fact that those benefits outweigh the costs of explicitly and directly constraining exports through government action.

What about the commonly claimed costs of *allowing* exports? This [viewpoint] will show that integrating U.S. markets with global ones is as likely to tamp volatility as it is to increase it; that the gains to energy-intensive manufacturing from constraining natural gas exports would be much smaller than the economic opportunities that would be lost; that allowing natural gas exports would likely curb rather than increase global greenhouse gas emissions; and that whether natural gas will be used to replace oil in U.S. cars and trucks depends little on whether exports are allowed. But the [viewpoint] also offers warnings on two fronts. Natural gas exports would slightly raise U.S. natural gas prices, with disproportionate consequences for low-income consumers. (Increased tax revenues due to exports should be used to mitigate that effect insofar as possible.) Local environmental risks arising from natural gas production would also rise due to new production for exports. This can, in principle, be safely managed, but that is not inevitable; the prospect of exports should lead industry and regulators to redouble their efforts. This last factor is particularly important: as the controversy over the Key-

stone XL pipeline demonstrated, export-oriented resource extraction may be particularly vulnerable to local and
environmental opposition; if allowing LNG exports were to
lead to a backlash against natural gas production in general,
the economic fallout could be vast. Conversely, if prudent
regulation of natural gas extraction in the public interest
raises natural gas prices and, as a result, makes some exports
uneconomic, that should be accepted as a desirable outcome.

The United States Should Allow
Gas Exports

In light of this analysis, I propose that the United States allow
LNG exports. In conjunction with this, the U.S. should take
other steps to mitigate potential downsides and leverage these
exports to its advantage.

The United States should approve applications to export
LNG from the United States, several of which are currently
pending, and more of which can be expected in the future.
This does not mean that the U.S. government should encourage exports *per se*; it should simply allow them to occur if
properly regulated markets steer the economy in that direction.

U.S. law distinguishes between LNG exports to countries
with which the United States has relevant free trade agreements (FTAs), which are fast-tracked for approval, and exports to other countries, which face more rigorous review and
must be judged to be consistent with the U.S. national interest. Some have argued that this distinction should be abol-
ished, since it interferes with free trade. The United States
should maintain the distinction, which can give it leverage in
trade negotiations without entailing any economic costs.

U.S. natural gas exports can also provide a platform for
more effective U.S. foreign and trade policy. To that end, the
United States should use foreign access to U.S. gas exports as

leverage in trade negotiations, and actively seek to steer global gas trade toward greater transparency and market-based pricing. . . .

A revolution in U.S. natural gas production has forced policy makers to decide whether they should allow exports of LNG from the United States. They should say yes, within prudent limits, and leverage U.S. exports for broader gain. Yet the mere fact that the benefits of allowing exports would outweigh the costs does not mean that the political fight over allowing LNG exports will be tame. Operators of natural gas power plants will likely oppose exports, as will energy-intensive manufacturers, though chemicals producers, if they are sufficiently enlightened, may take a more moderate stance. Most environmental advocates who are concerned with the local impacts of shale gas development will likely join in opposition, as will those who are convinced that gas should be tapped for use in cars and trucks, and those who believe that any rise in consumer energy prices is unacceptable. The most prominent proponents of exports will likely be oil and gas companies and advocates of liberal trade, perhaps along with a broader group of foreign policy strategists that finds the prospect of disrupting relations between gas-producing and gas-consuming countries appealing, as well as supporters of renewable power who see cheap natural gas as competition. Any decision on LNG exports is likely to be controversial. Enlightened leadership and a strategy that mitigates downsides for poorer consumers and the local environment are essential to a smart strategy for constructively moving exports forward.

"Gas exports would transform the energy landscape and communities across the country. . . . We need to look before we leap."

Exporting Natural Gas Will Pollute the Environment

Craig Segall

Craig Segall is staff attorney for the Sierra Club's Environmental Law Program. In the following viewpoint, Segall explains that fracking has created a boom in natural gas production, making it possible for the United States to export as much as 45 percent of its current domestic production. The Department of Energy has the authority to approve gas exports, but so far it has failed to fully investigate the environmental impact of substantially increasing gas production, he asserts. Segall argues that because of the significant threats to air and water quality that large-scale fracking could create, it is essential that a full environmental impact statement be prepared.

As you read, consider the following questions:

1. What are some of the environmental considerations from fracking, according to the author?

2. What are some of the climate policy implications of natural gas exports, according to the author?

3. What benefits does the author see coming from a National Environmental Policy Act environmental impact statement?

Exporting American natural gas to the world market would spur unconventional natural gas production across the country, increasing pollution and disrupting landscapes and communities. Deciding whether to move forward is among the most pressing environmental and energy policy decisions facing the nation. Yet, as the Department of Energy (DOE) considers whether to green-light gas exports of as much as 45% of current U.S. gas production—more gas than the entire domestic power industry burns in a year—it has refused to disclose, or even acknowledge, the environmental consequences of its decisions. In fact, DOE has not even acknowledged that its own National Energy Modeling System can be used to help develop much of this information, instead preferring to turn a blind eye to the problem. DOE needs to change course. Even much smaller volumes of export have substantial environmental implications and exporting a large percentage of the total volume proposed would greatly affect the communities and ecosystems across America. The public and policy makers deserve, and are legally entitled to, a full accounting of these impacts.

Fracking Threatens Air and Water Quality

Gas exports are only possible because of the unconventional natural gas boom which hydraulic fracturing ("fracking") has unlocked. DOE's own advisory board has warned of the boom's serious environmental impacts. DOE is charged with determining whether such exports are in the public interest despite the damage that would result. To do that, it needs a full accounting of the environmental impacts of increasing gas production significantly to support exports.

These environmental considerations include significant threats to air and water quality from the industry's wastes, and the industrialization of entire landscapes. Gas production is associated with significant volumes of highly contaminated wastewater and the risk of groundwater contamination; it has also brought persistent smog problems to entire regions, along with notable increases in toxic and carcinogenic air pollutants. Regulatory measures to address these impacts have been inadequate, meaning that increased production very likely means increased environmental harm. Natural gas exports also have important climate policy implications on several fronts: Even if exported gas substitutes for coal abroad (which it may or may not do), it will not produce emissions reductions sufficient to stabilize the climate, and gas exports will increase our investment in fossil fuels. Moreover, the gas export process is particularly carbon intensive, and gas exports will likely raise gas prices domestically, increasing the market share of dirty coal power, meaning that perceived climate benefits may be quite limited if they exist at all. The upshot is that increasing gas production comes with significant domestic costs.

An Environmental Impact Statement Is Needed

The National Environmental Policy Act (NEPA) process is designed to generate just such an analysis. NEPA analyses, properly done, provide full, fair, descriptions of a project's environmental implications, remaining uncertainties, and alternatives that could avoid environmental damage. A full NEPA environmental impact statement looking programmatically at export would help DOE and the public fairly weigh these proposals' costs and benefits, and to work with policy makers at the federal, state, and local levels to address any problems. In fact, the U.S. Environmental Protection Agency has repeatedly

Exporting Fracked Gas Will Hurt the Environment

If you want to know just how bad an idea it is for America to ship "fracked" natural gas to overseas markets, travel the 65 miles from the White House to a place called Cove Point in southern Maryland. . . .

The Cove Point plant in Maryland is just one of more than 20 such "liquefaction" plants now proposed—but not yet built—for coastal areas nationwide. . . .

This gas needs to stay in the ground. If it's dug up and exported, it will directly harm just about everyone in the U.S. economy while simultaneously making global warming worse.

Bill McKibben and Mike Tidwell, "A Big Fracking Lie,"
Politico Magazine, January 21, 2014.

called for just such an analysis. Without one, America risks committing itself to a permanent role as a gas supplier to the world without determining whether it can do so safely while protecting important domestic interests.

Equally troublingly, even as DOE has thus far failed to fulfill its obligation to protect the public interest by weighing environmental impacts, it risks losing its authority altogether. A drafting quirk in the export licensing statute intended to speed gas imports from Canada means that DOE must grant licenses for gas exports to nations with which the United States has signed a free trade agreement which includes national treatment of natural gas. This rubber stamp applies even if the proposed exports would not otherwise be in the public interest. As the U.S. negotiates a massive trade agreement which may include nations hungry for U.S. exports, the Trans-Pacific

Partnership, this mandatory rubber stamp risks undercutting DOE's ability to protect the public.

The bottom line is that before committing to massive gas exports, federal decision makers need to ensure that they, and the public, have the environmental information they need to make a fair decision, and the authority to do so. That means ensuring that a full environmental impact statement discloses exports' impacts and develops alternatives to reduce them. It also means defending DOE's prerogatives against the unintended effects of trade pacts. Congress and the U.S. trade negotiators must ensure that agreements like the Trans-Pacific Partnership are designed to maintain DOE's vital public interest inquiry.

Gas exports would transform the energy landscape and communities across the country. We owe ourselves an open national conversation to test whether they are in the public interest. We need to look before we leap.

| *"We should believe what markets tell us."*

Banning Natural Gas Exports Will Not Address Environmental and Economic Concerns

Ed Dolan

Ed Dolan is an economist and educator who has taught at Dartmouth College, George Mason University, and the University of Chicago. He also has worked as an economist for the antitrust division of the US Department of Justice. In the following viewpoint, Dolan examines the arguments of those opposing the exporting of US natural gas and calls these arguments unconvincing because they are too narrowly focused. As an example, Dolan says that large-scale users of gas focus only on the impact of gas exports on gas-using industries instead of their impact on the larger economy. What is needed, he maintains, is a broad reexamination of all of the nation's environmental and energy policies.

As you read, consider the following questions:

1. What flaws does the author find in the argument that gas exports would lead to skyrocketing prices?

2. How does the author address the concern that any increase in gas prices will disproportionally impact low-income families?

3. What arguments do environmentalists make against gas exports, and how does the author respond to them?

The energy policy topic of the week [of May 9, 2013] is whether to export more of America's newly abundant natural gas. Like any good card-carrying economist, my instincts favor free trade. Other things being equal, that makes me pro-export. Still, shouldn't we listen to what the other side has to say? Maybe gas is different. Maybe exporting it is not such a good idea after all. So just how strong is the case against permitting more natural gas exports?

Would Low Gas Prices Strengthen the U.S. Economy?

Large users of natural gas are among the most vocal opponents of increased exports. Not surprisingly, they argue that today's gas prices, still only a little above their historic lows, are a boon for the U.S. economy. Speaking recently [in February 2013] to *Politico*, Andrew Liveris, CEO [chief executive officer] of Dow Chemical, put it this way:

> [w]hen natural gas is not solely used as an export, and is used as a building block for manufactured goods, it creates eight times more value across the entire economy. In this way, America's natural gas bounty is more than a simple commodity. It's a once-in-a-generation opportunity to export advanced products and not just BTUs [British thermal units].

Unfortunately, pointing out that we could use any exported primary good to make advanced products at home instead does not, by itself, tell us much about whether it should be exported. Existing trade patterns suggest that the United States sometimes has a comparative advantage in exporting primary goods and sometimes more highly processed ones. For example, we export more wheat than pasta, but we import primary aluminum and export aircraft. There is no general rule that says exporting advanced products is the path to prosperity.

We should believe what markets tell us. If they tell us we can't profitably export certain advanced chemical products without imposing barriers to overseas sales of natural gas, that probably means we should be exporting the gas. Forcing exports uphill against market fundamentals only makes us poorer in the long run.

Would Gas Exports Lead to Skyrocketing Prices?

The fear of higher prices is another favorite argument of those who oppose gas exports. The *Financial Times* quotes Peter Huntsman, chief executive of Huntsman chemicals, as saying, "If all the proposed gas export projects were built with reckless abandonment . . . then the U.S. price of gas would skyrocket." We could "wake up tomorrow and find we have a flat gas price internationally," he warns.

Since natural gas currently sells for $18 per thousand cubic feet (Mcf) in Japan and $12 per Mcf in Europe, compared with prices that have recently been as low as $2 per Mcf in the United States, the prospect of international parity for gas prices does look frightening. For three reasons, however, the actual effects on U.S. prices are likely to be far from full equalization.

First, no one expects U.S. prices to stay at $2 per Mcf over the long term. Prices have already rebounded to over $4 per

Mcf. Michael Levi, who has studied gas exports for the Hamilton Project, uses $5 per Mcf as a consensus estimate for U.S. domestic prices in the medium term, not taking the impact of exports into account.

Second, it is expensive to ship gas from the United States to Asia or Europe. There are no transatlantic or transpacific pipelines; the gas has to move in liquid form, as LNG [liquefied natural gas]. Levi estimates costs of liquefaction, transportation, and regasification to be about $5 per Mcf. That means foreign prices are likely to stay at least that much higher than U.S. prices for the foreseeable future.

Third, gas prices in many parts of the world are currently high because they are linked to the price of oil. That link has now been broken in the United States, where it also once held. It is likely that large-scale U.S. exports would undermine the oil-gas link in the rest of the world. If so, exports would cause foreign prices to fall at the same time they put upward pressure on U.S. prices.

When all is said and done, it seems unlikely that U.S. gas prices would rise by more than 10 to 20 percent even with unrestricted exports, while U.S. users of gas would retain at least a $5 per Mcf advantage over foreign competitors. That ought to be enough to establish a comparative advantage for U.S. producers of many gas-based chemical products, especially where transportation costs relative to value are lower for advanced products than for the gas itself.

Some observers also worry that even a small increase in gas prices would disproportionately impact low-income families. For example, Levi estimates that a $1 per Mcf increase in gas prices would cost $50 per year for a family with $20,000 of income, but proportionately less—about $90 per year—for a family with $100,000 of income. On the face of it, however, that strikes me as a weak argument in favor of restricting exports. Taking Levi's estimates at face value, it is clear that the great bulk of the consumer benefits of low gas prices accrue

Lifting the Export Ban Makes Economic Sense

Exporting natural gas and oil does not increase America's dependence on foreign imports (which mostly come from nations outside the Middle East). Selling oil would merely reshuffle global supplies, giving American producers the most money for the best product. . . .

Lifting the export prohibition would have little impact on consumer prices. The ban most directly benefits refiners, who are *exporting record amounts of products*, than American consumers. Studies suggest that eliminating the ban would result in at most only modest price increases. . . .

Trying to artificially hold down prices always has been bad energy policy. For years Washington imposed arbitrary energy controls. Below market prices encouraged consumption and discouraged production. That was a stupid policy then. It is an equally stupid policy now.

Doug Bandow, "Free America's Energy Future: Drop Washington's Counterproductive Oil and Natural Gas Export Ban," Forbes, January 27, 2014.

to middle- and upper-income families. It would be far more cost-effective to offset any distributional impact of gas prices by means of an expansion of targeted programs, such as the existing Low Income Home Energy Assistance Program, than through the blunt instrument of export restrictions.

Would Gas Exports Harm the Environment?

The chemical industry has been the most vocal element of the coalition opposing natural gas exports, but environmentalists are an important junior partner. Recently [March 11, 2013] a group of environmental organizations, headed by the Sierra Club, sent a letter to President [Barack] Obama urging a time-out on natural gas export permits. The letter points to the potential environmental harms of increased U.S. natural gas production, including increased local air and water pollution from hydraulic fracturing, and to adverse impacts on climate change.

The concerns are real, but an export moratorium for natural gas is a clumsy and possibly counterproductive way to address them. In an earlier post [May 4, 2012] on the economics of fracking, I agreed that local air and water pollution from fracking are problems that need attention. Necessary measures include regulations to ensure that all operators follow industry best practices, regulatory and legal mechanisms to ensure that operators compensate parties harmed by local pollution, and further research into methods for mitigating adverse environmental effects. However, we should undertake all of those measures whether we use the gas produced by fracking domestically or export it.

If environmental organizations can make tactical use of the export controversy to secure greater efforts to mitigate the adverse effects of fracking, more power to them. However, that is no reason to make the export ban an end in itself. In fact, strengthening U.S. regulations on fracking and then exporting the resulting gas could well be better for the global environment than would be a policy that encouraged fracking in countries where regulations are weaker.

Similarly, a ban on gas exports is a poor tool for addressing the problem of climate change. As I have often argued, we could best address climate change in the context of an energy policy that promoted conservation and low-carbon alternatives by imposing emission charges for greenhouse gasses on all energy users and producers.

The Sierra Club letter makes the claim that natural gas exports would accelerate climate change. It cites a life-cycle analysis by Paula Jaramillo and colleagues at Carnegie Mellon University that challenges the reputation of LNG as a low-carbon fuel when methane leakages and energy used in transportation are taken into account. Other studies, like that of Michael Levi, cited above, argue that exported LNG would displace enough coal to produce a modest net reduction in global greenhouse gas emissions.

Regardless of which studies are right, an appropriate charge for greenhouse gas emissions remains the optimal solution. If further research shows that climate impact of LNG exports is near the high end of the (wide) range given in the Jaramillo study, and that the climate impact of coal is near the lower end of the range, a carbon charge could render natural gas exports uneconomic. We would then know that gas exports are not a good idea after all. However, short-circuiting the process by banning exports *a priori* [based on presumptive reasoning] is not the right approach.

The Bottom Line

When it comes down to it, the strategy of the anti-export lobby is to frame the issue as narrowly as possible: Focus on wages and profits in gas-using industries without looking at effects on the broader economy; bring in distributional effects without asking whether there is a better way to help the poor; and mobilize grassroots opposition to fracking without questioning the perversity of an energy policy that encourages waste by holding domestic prices as low as possible. Indications are that these efforts will fall short. The White House seems on the verge of approving new export permits. Let's hope that is just the first step in a comprehensive rethink of all of our energy and environmental policies.

| "The Department of Energy should move forward on all export applications in a timely manner."

Exporting Natural Gas Is in the National Interest

Lisa Murkowski

Lisa Murkowski is the senior US senator from the state of Alaska. She serves as ranking member of the Senate Committee on Energy and Natural Resources. In the following viewpoint, she explains that advances in technology have substantially increased the supply of natural gas in America, creating a surplus by 2020 that will make exporting gas possible. Several applications to export natural gas are awaiting approval by the US Department of Energy, the senator reports, recommending that the department approve them all in a timely manner. An examination of the pros and cons of exporting natural gas by a number of research institutions has concluded that these exports would produce economic benefits and that domestic gas prices would not increase significantly as a result, Murkowski maintains.

As you read, consider the following questions:

1. What are some of the ways the United States and other countries are increasing their use of natural gas, according to Murkowski?

Lisa Murkowski, "The Narrowing Window: America's Opportunity to Join the Global Gas Trade," US Senate Committee on Energy and Natural Resources, August 6, 2013.

2. What three factors does the senator argue are presenting the United States with "a historic opportunity to increase its exports of natural gas"?

3. Murkowski argues that by exporting natural gas, the United States will help some of its allies. How does she say this will happen?

Proved reserves of natural gas have increased every year since 1998. The Energy Information Administration (EIA), the independent statistical agency of the Department of Energy, produces an estimate, updated annually, of proved reserves of dry natural gas. From 2000 to 2010, that estimate increased from 177.4 trillion cubic feet (tcf) to 304.6 tcf. This increase of over 70 percent was largely due to technological advances made in hydraulic fracturing and horizontal drilling, which made shale gas economic to produce.

The Growing Resource Base

While proved reserves have grown dramatically, so have estimates of unproved natural gas resources. The EIA's estimates increased approximately 50 percent from 1999 to 2009, rising from 1,330.9 tcf to 1,903.7 tcf. These numbers include what are referred to as "undiscovered resources" and do not factor in economic feasibility.

Advances in technology allowing access to the vast unconventional gas resources are driving these dramatic increases. In 1999, the EIA estimated that unproved unconventional gas resources stood at 358.0 tcf, from a combination of shale, coal bed methane, and other types of rock. In 2009, the EIA's estimate of unproved unconventional gas resources grew to 1,026.7 tcf, an increase of 186.8 percent.

Some caution is warranted when discussing these numbers: assessment methodologies change over time, terminology evolves, and different analyses yield different results. When EIA makes estimates it assumes the status quo for technology, policy, and other factors. It is telling, nonetheless, that official U.S. government estimates are aligned in both magnitude and trend with other highly respected assessments, such as the Potential Gas Committee's biennial estimate of U.S. natural gas resources. From 2002 to 2012, its estimate of the future gas supply, which includes both potential resources and proved reserves, increased from 1,314 tcf to 2,688 tcf. This is an increase of more than 100 percent.

It is also true that even these expanded projections may ultimately prove to be dramatically understated. Collaborating scientists from the United States and Japan are currently examining the potential of methane hydrates as an energy source. These are deposits in Arctic and deepwater marine environments where natural gas has been trapped in place by frozen water molecules. Extracting this gas efficiently and safely is challenging. However, recent breakthroughs suggest that commercial-scale production may one day be technically and economically possible. Research is ongoing and continually improving. According to the Bureau of Ocean Energy Management, approximately 21,444 tcf of methane hydrate resources exist in the Gulf of Mexico alone. There are also significant methane hydrate resources on Alaska's North Slope and offshore. If research efforts are ultimately successful, methane hydrates will increase the resource base exponentially.

A genuine energy revolution is under way. Technology will increase the magnitude of these resources and economics will render more of them accessible to industry. The geological component of the U.S. natural gas bounty is undeniable and threats to supply will emanate above ground, from legislative and regulatory intervention, not below it.

The Coming Surplus

This vast resource base has facilitated dramatic increases in domestic natural gas production. The U.S. surpassed Russia as the world's largest natural gas producer in 2009. The number of natural gas exploration and development wells also rose to record levels in the 2004–2008 period, leading to a boom in production. The sustained nature of this rise is critical, not the peak of any particular year. In 2012, the U.S. produced about 24.1 tcf of natural gas, the highest level on record.

The U.S. currently consumes more natural gas than it produces, making it a net importer. According to EIA, in 2012 the nation consumed approximately 25.5 tcf of natural gas. The geography of the North American continent enables the U.S. to export gas in significant quantities by pipeline to Canada and Mexico. Canada supplied the bulk of U.S. imports as the two markets are highly integrated. Some imports in the form of liquefied natural gas (LNG) came from Qatar, Trinidad and Tobago, and occasionally other countries. These imports have filled the gap between production and consumption.

Most North American gas is retained within North America. The U.S. is a net importer from Canada, with which it has a particularly close relationship. In a report subtitled "Joined at the Well," the Congressional Research Service states that the two countries "effectively comprise a single integrated market." In fact, gas pipelines cross the border at dozens of points in the Northwest, Midwest, and Northeast. The U.S. is a net exporter to Mexico. Gas exports from the U.S. to both neighbors are at record highs—971 billion cubic feet (bcf) to Canada and 620 bcf to Mexico in 2012—while gas imports from Canada are at their lowest level since 1997.

Although the U.S. is currently a net importer of natural gas, its trade balance in this respect is improving rapidly. Net imports have fallen every year since 2007 and are currently at their lowest levels since 1990. The EIA projects that production will exceed consumption in 2019, which would result in a surplus of natural gas. Some of this surplus will be exported by pipeline to Canada and, increasingly, to Mexico, while the remainder will be liquefied and exported overseas.

The EIA is not alone in this projection. In its "Global Trends 2030" publication, the National Intelligence Council forecasts that "the US could emerge as a major energy exporter" by 2020, partly as a result of "substantial global exports" of natural gas. The International Energy Agency projects that the U.S. "emerges as an LNG exporter before 2020," but cautions that those exports will be "fairly limited." Low levels of LNG have already in the past been exported to Japan or reexported to an array of other countries, including Brazil, while imports have fallen by more than 77 percent since 2007.

Exports are possible without a domestic surplus of natural gas. Yet it is the coming surplus that will facilitate the expansion of the U.S. natural gas trade beyond the North American integrated pipeline network and onto tankers across the world. Pipelines are regional, but LNG is global, and it is in the interest of the United States to pursue this global opportunity.

A Growing Global Trade

The global natural gas resource base is enormous. At current rates of usage, it could well last centuries, not decades.

Natural gas resources in large regions of the world have not been adequately assessed for a variety of reasons, but geologists can make useful estimates based on existing information and technology. In 2012, the U.S. Geological Survey reported that undiscovered, technically recoverable conventional gas resources outside the United States stood at approximately 5,606 tcf. Separately, the EIA estimated global, unproved, technically recoverable shale gas resources to be 6,634 tcf, excluding the U.S. The total global resource base would include these numbers, as well as additional trillions of cubic feet from proved reserves and resource growth, and may grow substantially as technology improves.

Natural gas is widely distributed across the globe. There are basins in North America, Australia, South America, Eastern Europe, Western Europe, Africa, and Asia. Individual formations estimated to hold more than 100 tcf of natural gas can be found in the United States, Canada, Mexico, Australia, Colombia and Venezuela, Argentina, Brazil, Poland, Russia, France, Algeria, South Africa, China, and Pakistan.

The prevalence of this resource is leading many countries, including the United States, to increase their usage of natural gas in various sectors of the economy. Natural gas vehicles, gas-fueled power plants, and other sources of demand continue to grow. In its "World Energy Outlook 2011," the International Energy Agency asked: "Are we entering a golden age of gas?" This scenario would be characterized by a world in which global demand for natural gas reaches new heights and is matched by rising global production from diverse regions of the world. The following year, the IEA noted: "The world's resources of natural gas are large enough to accommodate vigorous expansion of demand for several decades."

A global gas market is developing to facilitate this rapid increase in both supply and demand. These trade flows are primarily via pipeline. According to BP's "Statistical Review of World Energy 2013," approximately 25 tcf of natural gas was traded globally by pipeline last year. Every region of the world participated in this pipeline trade, although most of the interest resided in North America and Europe. LNG exports are also contributing a larger portion to the total gas trade. Approximately 11.6 tcf of LNG was traded via tanker in 2012, most of which was ultimately imported by countries in Asia and Western Europe. At present, relatively few countries are able to participate in the LNG trade. LNG export leaders, ranked in descending order, include Qatar, Malaysia, Australia, Nigeria, Indonesia, Algeria, Oman, Brunei, the United Arab Emirates, and Yemen. Smaller amounts of exports flow from Equatorial Guinea and Egypt. It is costly to liquefy natural gas and load it onto tankers. Export facilities also take years to construct and typically entail contracts with importing customers that span decades. Expensive infrastructure to convert

LNG back into gaseous form is also a limitation on market participants. Japan and South Korea, alone, account for half of the world's LNG imports.

Global demand for LNG is rising. Tankers can transport gas to any suitable port in the world, while pipelines are obviously more limited. The IEA projects that the size of the LNG trade will grow over 75 percent by 2035 and that the total export capacity of LNG projects around the world will rise to nearly 17 tcf by approximately 2018. Although future utilization rates and LNG demand are uncertain, it is clear that market forces will shape the development of the network of export and import terminals.

The Opportunity

The combination of three factors—a vast domestic resource base, production outpacing demand (leading to a surplus), and a burgeoning global market—presents the United States with a historic opportunity to increase its exports of natural gas.

The relevant regulatory process is, in theory, straightforward. In order to export natural gas, a project must apply for authorization from the Department of Energy. Exports to countries with which the U.S. has a free trade agreement, known as FTA countries, are authorized automatically. Exports to non-FTA countries require a review by DOE, which must approve all applications unless they can be positively demonstrated to run counter to the public interest. Most of the growing demand for LNG emanates from non-FTA countries, which means that in practice all export terminals require DOE approval. The Federal Energy Regulatory Commission (FERC) is also mandated to permit onshore LNG terminals, including conducting environmental review in accordance with the National Environmental Policy Act. The Department of Transportation's Maritime Administration is mandated to license each offshore LNG terminal.

Predictions That the World Is Entering a "Golden Age of Gas"

- Natural gas is projected to play an increasingly important role in the global energy economy. It is the only fossil fuel for which demand rises in all three "Outlook" scenarios. In the New Policies Scenario, world demand increases to 4.75 tcm [trillion cubic meters] in 2035 at an average rate of 1.7% per year. Global gas consumption catches up with coal consumption. Gas demand growth in the Current Policies Scenario is 2% per year, pulled up by higher total energy demand, but is only 0.9% in the 450 Scenario as demand peaks around 2030, before falling in favour of zero-carbon energy sources.

- Economic growth and energy policies in non-OECD [Organisation for Economic Co-operation and Development] countries will be the key determinant of future gas consumption: non-OECD countries account for 81% of demand growth in the New Policies Scenario. A major expansion of gas use in China pushes domestic demand above 500 bcm [billion cubic meters] by 2035, from 110 bcm in 2010. Power generation takes the largest share of global consumption, increasing at 1.8% per year in the New Policies Scenario; but there is a broad-based rise in gas use across industry, buildings and (from a much lower base) also the transportation sectors.

International Energy Agency,
"World Energy Outlook 2011," 2011.

Existing infrastructure that was originally constructed to facilitate the importing of LNG from other countries can be converted into export facilities. Conversion of these "brown-field" projects can save billions of dollars when compared to the construction of brand-new export terminals, also known as "greenfield" projects. There are currently 11 import terminals. These are located in Georgia, Louisiana, Maryland, Massachusetts, Mississippi, Texas, and Puerto Rico. Applications to convert two of these projects into export facilities already have been approved by DOE for non-FTA countries.

Domestic natural gas prices in the U.S. are considerably lower than gas prices in other parts of the world. The Henry Hub price, which is the U.S. benchmark, is approximately $4 per MMBtu (million British thermal units). The price in Japan has been as high as $16–18 per MMBtu, while $9–10 per MMbtu is more the norm in Europe. Liquefaction of natural gas is an expensive process, however. The construction of facilities, the cooling and transportation of the gas, and the regasification all narrow the gap between U.S. and world prices. Despite these costs, a business opportunity remains.

In geopolitical terms, the build-out of LNG capacity also provides the U.S. an opportunity to provide relief to several of its allies. The mere entry of the U.S. into the global market will improve competition, reducing prices for importers. In fact, to some degree this has already begun. Imports of LNG from the U.S. will also enable other countries to diversify their sources of energy. Japan and India in particular, which do not have free trade agreements with the United States, have urged the federal government to approve LNG exports to those countries. Observers have also noted that American LNG would serve to reduce the leverage Russia can currently exert over Europe through its gas pipeline network. The argument is not that U.S. exports would necessarily replace Russian gas, but that clients of Russia would have a stronger negotiating position, as well as access to additional supply. LNG exports from the U.S. would also strengthen global resilience to turmoil in the Middle East, including the capacity of the international community to impose sanctions on Iran.

Certain interests have objected to the possibility of LNG exports from the U.S. Some petrochemical producers have argued that exports of natural gas would raise the domestic price of natural gas, undercutting their own businesses and product exports by raising the cost of their fuel and feedstock.

A robust debate occurred in the analytical community, comprising universities, think tanks, consultancies, and other research institutions. After months of discussion and analysis, the majority of reports concluded that LNG exports would provide net economic benefits to the U.S. and should be approved in a timely fashion. Virtually all of these reports concluded that the impact on domestic natural gas prices would be manageable and limited. In addition, many of these reports have found that higher domestic natural gas prices would also actually serve to increase (and stabilize) natural gas production in the U.S. by making it economical to produce additional natural gas resources. In other words, slightly higher domestic natural gas prices would lead to new production.

Furthermore, domestic consumers benefit from trade, too. First, exports result in wealth creation, which leads to investment and jobs at home. Second, long-term export contracts provide a steady source of demand at a predictable price. Overall export volumes will likely be a small fraction of national production, but can certainly contribute to the stabilization of prices by providing another aspect of certainty to the natural gas market. Consumers will gain from this reduction in volatility.

The analytical debate about whether exports are in the national interest is settled. Nonetheless, models are imperfect and cannot guarantee the future. Natural gas prices will certainly fluctuate in the coming decades. Ultimately, it is not the role of the federal government to decide which industries should prosper and which should falter, nor to attempt to set a band of "acceptable" domestic natural gas prices. Past history has shown that attempts by the federal government to control domestic prices have resulted in unintended consequences and negative impacts to the U.S. economy. The risks of building out LNG capacity are manageable, particularly for the government, while the potential gains to the nation's economy are enormous.

The Issue of Timing

The window for the United States to join the global gas trade will not be open indefinitely. In fact, it is narrowing, and there is a real possibility that the nation will miss out on a historic opportunity.

Global demand for LNG is growing but limited, and it is quickly being met by forthcoming supply. Current worldwide capacity is about 37 bcf per day, most of which lies in the Middle East and Asia. North American LNG export capacity is miniscule in comparison. Additional exports projects, totaling over 10 bcf per day, are already under construction in Algeria, Australia, Indonesia, and Papua New Guinea. In contrast, each project being considered in the U.S. can bring only 1–3 bcf per day of additional capacity. With additional projects in the planning stages in Qatar, Australia, Canada, and elsewhere, the world simply may not need LNG from the U.S. to meet new demand in the future. Consumers will have other options.

There is also a unique opportunity for Alaska, given that state's proximity to markets in Asia. Until this spring, the liquefaction facility at Kenai [Alaska] had been licensed to export small quantities of LNG to Japan since 1969. Before more substantial trade materializes, however, a major pipeline must be constructed from the North Slope, where the USGS [United States Geological Survey] estimates about 42 tcf of shale gas alone may be recovered, to the southern coast of Alaska. A larger liquefaction facility will also be required. A project proposed by BP, ConocoPhillips, ExxonMobil, and

TransCanada is estimated to cost between \$45–65 billion. Alaska will also face competition from projects overseas, in Canada, and in the continental United States.

The gap between U.S and world prices for natural gas will narrow in the coming years. As other suppliers come online, importers will pay less for the LNG they purchase. Other nations will be competing for long-term contracts, which are important for export approvals and necessary for securing long-term financing. The capacity of the financial markets to support such costly projects is not infinite and will serve to limit the number of projects that are ultimately built.

The narrow window that this creates is not confined to our nation. Potential LNG producers in other countries, such as Canada and Australia, have warned that projects in their own countries may miss opportunities. Delays in permitting, problems with construction, lack of financing, environmental and special interest opposition, and other issues can all negatively impact the feasibility of export facilities. We in government should do what we can to help alleviate those problems.

Recommendations

1. The Department of Energy should move forward on all export applications in a timely manner. DOE itself has already determined that exports of LNG are in the national interest. There may be valid reasons for the denial of certain applications, but this should not stop DOE from moving forward on other applications, reviewing them, and making final decisions. Artificial timetables, such as an arbitrary gap of six to eight weeks between decisions, should be avoided.

2. Any legislation requiring additional economic studies, more restrictive rulemaking at the Department of Energy, or any other policy that serves to delay or prohibit the exporting of liquefied natural gas should be opposed.

3. If the Department of Energy considers revisions to its application review procedures, any such modification should expedite, rather than delay, the process.

4. The development of natural gas resources should be a priority for the United States. Funding for research and development of unconventional gas resources, including methane hydrates, should be maintained or increased. Congress should also support efforts to streamline the permitting process for natural gas exploration, development, and production projects; reject attempts to increases taxes that make natural gas less viable to produce; and oppose efforts to make the regulatory process uncertain, inefficient, overly burdensome, or duplicative. This should include natural gas pipeline construction, maintenance, and rehabilitation projects.

5. Federal agencies with natural gas–related projects and programs overseas should collaborate to ensure there is no duplication of effort and that all policy goals are properly aligned.

"Proper, transparent mechanisms must be in place to effectively evaluate all LNG export applications—prior to their approval—to gauge whether each application is in the public interest."

Exporting Natural Gas Is Not in the National Interest

Ron Wyden

Ron Wyden is a senator from Oregon and chair of the US Senate Committee on Energy and Natural Resources. In the following viewpoint, Wyden points out that a study prepared by the National Economic Research Associates (NERA) Economic Consulting firm that was commissioned by the US Department of Energy is seriously flawed and should not be considered in the approval process for applications to export natural gas. The major problem with the study is that NERA used projections from the Energy Information Administration's 2011 annual energy outlook, instead of the 2013 outlook, according to the senator. The projections for gas consumption, energy prices, and electric-sector energy consumption are significantly different in the two reports, making the NERA study inaccurate, Wyden argues.

Ron Wyden, Letter to Steven Chu, Secretary, US Department of Energy, January 10, 2013.

As you read, consider the following questions:

1. According to Wyden, what are some of the data differences between the 2011 and 2013 annual energy outlooks?

2. What are some of the sources that will create domestic demand for additional natural gas over the next decade, according to Wyden?

3. What are some of the negative consequences of gas exports that the NERA report cites?

Dear Secretary [Steven] Chu:

After reviewing the recently released [December 2012] NERA [National Economic Research Associates] Economic Consulting study commissioned by the department, I remain deeply concerned about the Department of Energy's approval process for liquefied natural gas ("LNG") export applications. The Natural Gas Act ("NGA") requires the department to determine whether approving an application to export LNG is in the "public interest," and the department has indicated that this report will be central to the approval process for these applications. Export applications, which are typically for 20 years or more, and the associated LNG export terminals will reshape the North American natural gas market for years to come. The shortcomings of the NERA study are numerous and render this study insufficient for the department to use in any export determination. The NERA study would need to be updated with new EIA [Energy Information Administration] projections, more realistic market assumptions, regional impacts of the proposed actual export terminals, and evaluations of the actual impacts on consumers and businesses of exporting LNG.

The Study Relies on Outdated Information

The NERA study's most glaring shortfall is its reliance on two-year-old domestic energy market projections that diverge widely from the government's current understanding of future supply and demand. The study used the Energy Information Administration's (EIA) "Annual Energy Outlook 2011" [AEO2011] reference case, which was released in 2010, as the foundation for its own LNG study. However, on the same day the NERA study was released, the EIA issued its "Annual Energy Outlook" reference case for 2013 [AEO2013]. There are significant differences between the two EIA AEO reference cases, including projections for gas consumption, energy prices and electric sector energy consumption that render the NERA study inaccurate in reflecting the current sector conditions necessary to inform today's decision making. Among the most notable data differences are:

- *More homes and businesses will rely on natural gas–fired electricity*: U.S. net electricity generation by coal power plants in 2035 is projected to be 22.7% lower in AEO2013 than in AEO2011; a majority of this power will be replaced by natural gas–fired generation, which is 15.2% more in AEO2013 than AEO2011.

- *Overall natural gas consumption will be higher*: The AEO2013 predicts U.S. natural gas consumption will be 8% higher in 2035 than the AEO2011 figure used by NERA.

- *EIA assumed LNG would be imported*: Perhaps the most illustrative deviation between the two sets of data is that EIA still expected the U.S. to import LNG in its AEO2011 projections adding to U.S. supplies. The AEO2013 projects there will be net exports of LNG, reducing U.S. supplies.

The Study Understates Natural Gas Demand

Even if NERA were to use the new EIA projections, the model it employed for this study has additional deficiencies that would need to be addressed before it could be relied upon to serve as a basis for the statutory findings required by the Natural Gas Act. For example:

1. The NERA study evaluates dozens of scenarios representing different market conditions, but it does not consider the significant domestic demand growth that outside experts and private industry expect to occur over the next decade. By excluding these sources of demand, NERA, like the EIA's annual energy outlooks, is significantly understating demand from emerging segments of the natural gas market. Two overlooked examples are as follows:

   • *Natural gas is expected to become major transportation fuel*: Outside experts suggest EIA has greatly underestimated the use of natural gas by the transportation sector. Citi [GPS: Global Perspectives & Solutions] projected that heavy trucks alone could use 3.3 Bcf/d [billion cubic feet per day] of natural gas by 2020, displacing up to 600,000 barrels of diesel fuel every day. The Citi estimate is more than 20 times what EIA projected in its AEO2011, which, in turn, is one-fourth of the agency's AEO2013 projection. The railroad industry is also reported to be studying a switch to natural gas–fueled locomotives, which would further drive up demand.

   • *Projected industrial growth is not fully accounted for by EIA or NERA*: The growth in natural gas production and low prices have attracted 100 proposed industrial projects, representing $90 billion in investment and tens of thousands of new jobs, according to Dow Chemical. The proposed projects identified in the Dow analysis represent an estimated increase in demand of 8 Bcf/d. Dow expects near-term industrial demand growth to reach 11 Bcf/d. The AEO2011 does not account for these projects, nor does the AEO2013. EIA actually projects non-electric related industrial natural gas demand to decline.

2. The NERA study purports to treat the U.S. and Canada as a single North American market, but its assumptions ignore the potential effect of Canadian LNG exports. The study ignores this important market development, even though Canada's National Energy Board has already approved two LNG export projects in British Columbia. The board also is considering a third LNG export project submitted over the summer by Royal Dutch Shell [commonly known as Shell]. Published reports suggest these projects could result in 9 billion cubic feet per day of exports, beginning as early as 2014.

3. LNG terminals use a substantial amount of energy in the liquefaction process. This energy is largely derived from natural gas, representing an amount equivalent to as much as 10% of the amount of natural gas ultimately processed into LNG during the conversion. Both the EIA and NERA appear to have misrepresented the use of natural gas by LNG terminals for this purpose, which in turn understates the overall gas demand attributable to LNG exports:

- *EIA understated natural gas consumption by LNG terminals*: In its analysis of LNG exports released in January 2012, the EIA reduced the amount of LNG that would actually be exported under its projections by 10% to account for this additional consumption of natural gas during conversion. (NERA uses the same low and high export cases of 6 Bcf and 12 Bcf.) Under the EIA's 6 Bcf/D export case, only 5.4 Bcf/D would actually be exported; in its 12 Bcf/D case, only 10.8 Bcf/D would actually be exported. DOE export permits are for actual export quotas. Thus, actual exports at those nominal 6 Bcf/D and 12 Bcf/D levels would require adding 10% to overall natural gas demand above and beyond the export volumes. The EIA analysis subtracts the gas used for processing.

- *The NERA study also underestimates LNG terminal demand*: The NERA study states that 9% of the LNG produced at the terminals will be "burned off" for liquefaction, which is likely a mischaracterization of the actual gas usage for liquefaction. High-value LNG would not be used to power the conversion plant. While there will be some boil-off losses after LNG is produced, the larger issue is the additional natural gas demand resulting from gas consumption during the liquefaction conversion process and how the NERA study factors this additional demand into the full exporting life-cycle process. Gas that is used for liquefaction, regardless of its source, needs to be added to the overall demand for natural gas attributable to export volumes approved in the export permits and placed on board LNG tankers. It does not appear that the NERA study does so. The NERA study further errs by pricing the cost of the additional conversion gas at the wellhead price of natural gas despite the fact that gas used for liquefaction will need to be processed and physically transported by pipeline to the LNG terminal location at higher cost and likely impacting transportation and hub and regional prices along the way.

Study Fails to Measure Economic Impacts

Although the NERA study acknowledges that some sectors of the economy will be hurt by exports, the NERA study fails to fully assess the impacts of rising natural gas prices on home-owners and businesses. The report recognizes negative consequences of LNG exports, but spends only a few paragraphs of its 230-page report actually examining them in detail. Still, they are notable:

- There is a massive wealth transfer between manufacturing and residential consumers that benefits the natural gas industry but "raises energy costs and, in the process, depresses both real wages and the return on capital in all other industries."

- Labor, investment and tax income would fall $10 billion in 2015 as a result of LNG exports; they are reduced by more than $30 billion in 2020 and more than $40 billion in 2025, 2030 and 2035.

- "Households will be negatively affected by having to pay higher prices for the natural gas they use for heating and cooking. Domestic industries for which natural gas is a significant component of their cost structure will experience increases in their cost of production, which will adversely impact their competitive position in a global market and harm U.S. consumers who purchase their goods."

- "In many regions and times of the year natural gas–fired generation sets the price of electricity so that increases in natural gas prices can impact electricity prices. These price increases will also propagate through the economy and affect both household energy bills and costs for businesses."

- With minimal analysis, the study concludes that a "narrow" group of energy-intensive, trade-exposed industries would experience "serious competitive impacts." The study tries to downplay the economic importance of these manufacturing industries by saying they represent ½% of total U.S. employment; however, that equaled 1.2 million jobs at the end of November. Given the number of current employees and future expected growth, these impacts deserve further study.

- Regional gas prices are expected to increase with higher demand and an increase in wellhead natural gas prices, leading to a decline in U.S. consumption of natural gas.

Despite these serious impacts that are acknowledged *within the study*, NERA has not conducted further in-depth inquiry into how these impacts will actually be felt in the economy. Appendix F of the study identifies a number of critical factors that the study simply did not consider, without which the report represents a wholly insufficient basis for approving individual export applications which will have significant national, regional and local impacts. These significant gaps in analysis are best explained by the text included in Appendix F itself:

- "*Where Production or Export Terminals Will Be Located*—There are proposals for export facilities in the Mid-Atlantic, Pacific Northwest, and Canada, all of which could change basis differentials and potentially the location of additional natural gas production, with corresponding regional impacts. To analyze alternative locations of export facilities it would be necessary to repeat both the EIA and the NERA analyses with additional scenarios incorporating demand for natural gas exports in different regions."

- "*Regional Economic Impacts*—Since EIA assumed that all demand for domestic production–associated LNG exports was located in the Gulf region, it was not possible in this study to examine regional impacts on either natural gas prices or economic activity. The Gulf coast is not necessarily a representative choice given the range of locations now in different applications, so that any attempt to estimate regional impacts would be misleading without more regional specificity in the location of exports."

- *"Effects on Different Socioeconomic Groups*—Changes in energy prices are often divided into 'effects on producers' and 'effects on consumers.' . . . The ultimate incidence of all price changes is on individuals and households, for private businesses are owned ultimately by people. Price changes affect not only the cost of goods and services purchased by households, but also their income from work and investments, transfers from government and the taxes they pay. More relevant indicators of the distribution of gains and losses include real disposable income by income category, real consumption expenditures by income category, and possibly other measures of distribution by socioeconomic group or geography. This study only addresses the net economic effects of natural gas price changes and improved export revenues, not their distribution."

As the department has acknowledged when it elected to insert the NERA study into the docket of each pending LNG export application, the department is statutorily required to assess the impact of the individual applications as well as the total impact of proposed export volumes. The NERA study provides no insight into the regional market impacts of these applications, and very little information on the effects of proposed exports on different socioeconomic groups. As such, it is not an adequate basis upon which to approve those individual applications.

As I stated in my previous letter, I remain deeply concerned that the department has not articulated a set of criteria or procedures that will allow it to meet its obligations under the Natural Gas Act to make the required public interest determinations. Proper, transparent mechanisms must be in

place to effectively evaluate all LNG export applications—
prior to their approval—to gauge whether each application is
in the public interest. The inadequacies of the NERA study
only underscore the need for the department to establish
those criteria and procedures in a transparent and accurate
manner informed by data that most accurately reflects the
world today.

| "By undercutting Russia's natural gas–based market power, more gas exports would further America's national security interests as well."

Want to Help the Ukrainian Opposition? Allow Natural Gas Exports

Josiah Neeley

Josiah Neeley is a policy analyst for the Armstrong Center for Energy and the Environment at the Texas Public Policy Foundation. In the following viewpoint, Neeley explains that a plentiful natural gas supply in the United States, unleashed by fracking, has driven down gas prices and has made exporting natural gas possible. Exporting natural gas to US allies could have important geopolitical benefits, he maintains. For example, Ukraine is currently dependent on Russia for natural gas, and Russia exploits this dependence for its own political purposes, Neeley contends. He concludes it would be in the national interest to export natural gas to countries such as Ukraine, making them less vulnerable to Russian exploitation.

As you read, consider the following questions:

1. What example does the author cite of Russia using its natural gas energy leverage as a political weapon?

2. According to the author, what is one of the reasons why gas prices have fallen in the United States but remain high in Europe and Japan?

3. What statistics does the author quote to support his argument that exporting natural gas would benefit the US economy?

After weeks of effort, a growing protest movement in Ukraine appears to be gaining traction. As with a similar series of demonstrations in 2005, which brought former prime minister Viktor Yushchenko to power, the protest movement is centered on whether the country will look to Russia or to Europe and the West as a model.

Whatever the results of the current demonstrations, breaking free of Russian dominance over the long term may prove a challenge for Ukraine. The country remains dependent on Russian natural gas as an energy source, and the Russian government has shown itself quite willing to use this energy leverage as a political weapon. In fact, Russia recently announced a deal to bolster the current pro-Russian Ukrainian government by providing loans and cheaper natural gas.

Ukrainian President Viktor Yanukovych has signed off on the agreement, which would cut the price of Russian natural gas by 30 percent, but the country's protesters are not backing down. Opposition leader Oleg Tyagnibok told the *Los Angeles Times* that the deal was "the price Moscow paid him for rejecting European integration," and the protests have continued unabated in Kiev.

Meanwhile, the United States is undergoing an unprecedented natural gas boom. Spurred by technological advances that have unlocked vast supplies of shale oil and gas, natural

© Pat Bagley/cagelcartoons.com.

gas prices have fallen over the past five years from a high of over $12 per million British thermal units (BTUs) to $4 per million BTUs. According to the Energy Information Administration, production is expected to increase an additional 56 percent by 2040.

Yet while prices have fallen in America, they remain high in Europe and Japan. Part of the reason for this disparity is a Bush administration–era regulation restricting the ability of companies to export natural gas. Under Executive Order (EO) 13337, companies wishing to build "facilities for the exportation or importation of petroleum, petroleum products, coal, or other fuels to or from a foreign country" must receive approval from the Department of Energy. Exceptions are made for countries that have a specific free trade agreement with the U.S.

This year the Obama administration granted approval to four export facilities for liquefied natural gas. And Secretary of Energy Ernest Moniz recently suggested that a related ban on oil exports should be repealed. Nearly 20 projects, however, are still awaiting DOE approval.

Allowing more exportation of natural gas would be a boon for the U.S. economy. A recent report by the American Council for Capital Formation found that approval of pending export facilities would increase U.S. GDP by between $15.6 billion and $73.6 billion and create as many as 452,300 jobs by 2035. And by undercutting Russia's natural gas–based market power, more gas exports would further America's national security interests as well.

> *"The United States could become a net exporter of natural gas by 2020 and will be 'almost self-sufficient in energy,' in net terms, by 2035.'"*

Exporting Natural Gas Will Benefit the US Economy

Scott Lincicome

Scott Lincicome is an international trade attorney, an adjunct scholar at the Cato Institute, and a visiting lecturer at Duke University. In the following viewpoint, Lincicome contends that the United States is ill-served by restrictions on natural gas exporting that were created at a time when the country was a net energy importer and dependent on fossil fuels. The United States is predicted to have a surplus of natural gas by 2020 and should change its licensing systems to allow for the exporting of gas, he argues. Restricting natural gas exports hurts the US economy and hinders domestic energy production, Lincicome concludes.

As you read, consider the following questions:

1. How does the author rebut the argument that increasing natural gas exports would lead to higher domestic prices?

2. How does the author respond to the argument that increasing natural gas exports would hurt the US economy?

3. Why does the author believe that current US export licensing requirements for natural gas and crude oil violate obligations under the General Agreement on Tariffs and Trade?

Revolutionary extraction technologies have helped increase the supply of fossil fuels in the United States, driving down prices, spurring economic activity, and potentially reversing the longtime status of the United States as a net energy importer to a significant exporter. Impeding that transition are outdated federal regulations—in particular discretionary export licensing systems for natural gas and crude oil—that restrict exports, distort domestic energy prices, deter investment, and encourage graft. They also subvert some of the [Barack] Obama administration stated policy objectives and could run afoul of U.S. international trade obligations.

Despite the potential economic windfall, opposition to exporting natural gas and crude oil has materialized among certain domestic consuming industries and environmental groups, causing the administration to delay any approvals on pending export-license applications. But there are compelling reasons to approve those applications and to overhaul our disjointed, anachronistic, export license systems to properly reflect the new energy landscape. . . .

The New American Energy Landscape

Fossil fuel extraction technologies, such as hydraulic fracturing ("fracking") and horizontal drilling have revolutionized the U.S. energy market. According to the U.S. Energy Information Administration, domestic production of crude oil and natural gas has skyrocketed in recent years and is projected to stay at relatively high levels for decades, even assuming existing state and federal restrictions on production and transport. As summarized by economist Mark Perry, "U.S. oil production reached a 15-year high in 2012 with a yearly increase that was the largest in history, net oil imports fell to a 21-year low, and U.S. energy self-sufficiency rose to a 22-year high last year."

The production spike has driven down domestic gas and oil prices, creating a significant gap between U.S. and international market prices. . . . [Natural] gas prices in Japan, the world's largest liquefied natural gas (LNG) consumer, were more than five times higher than U.S. prices in 2012, and European prices were three to four times higher.

The increase in domestic energy supplies and resulting decline in prices has been a boon to downstream industries, such as electricity generators and petrochemical producers that rely on fossil fuels for energy or feedstock. According to the Boston Consulting Group, low energy prices have contributed, and will continue to contribute, to an American "manufacturing renaissance" in terms of domestic employment and export competitiveness in these sectors.

The resulting price differentials have U.S. energy producers positioned to become a global exporting powerhouse, and could reverse the United States' historic position as a net energy importer. According to a November 2012 report by the International Energy Agency [IEA], the United States could become a net exporter of natural gas by 2020 and will be "almost self-sufficient in energy, in net terms, by 2035." That same report estimates that the United States will become the world's largest oil producer by around 2020, causing North America to emerge as a net oil exporter by 2035.

Fossil Fuel Export Restrictions and Pending Applications

It would be difficult for those market projections to materialize under the current regulatory environment. In particular, natural gas and crude oil exports continue to be governed by licensing systems adopted when the United States was a net energy importer and dependent on fossil fuels for energy production—a picture far different from the production, price, and trade realities that exist today.

The U.S. government regulates natural gas imports and exports under the Natural Gas Act of 1938 and its amendments. Under the current law, all natural gas exports must be authorized by the Department of Energy (DOE), and authorization will be granted unless exportation "will not be consistent with the public interest." Exports to free trade agreement (FTA) partner countries are deemed to be consistent with the public interest, and DOE must therefore grant license applications "without modification or delay" when the customer is in a country that is an FTA partner.

Exports to non-FTA partners are presumed to be in the public interest, but this presumption can be rebutted with evidence that the exports would be inconsistent with the public interest. Neither U.S. law nor agency practice establishes binding, objective criteria that DOE must apply when determining whether an export license application meets the public-interest requirement. Moreover, DOE has explained repeatedly that, while it has developed various criteria for evaluating an application, the agency retains complete discretion when deciding whether to grant a license. For example, in a December 2012 letter to U.S. senator Ron Wyden (D-OR), DOE listed the criteria that it applies: (i) domestic need for the natural gas proposed for export; (ii) adequacy of domestic natural gas supply; (iii) U.S. energy security; (iv) impact on the U.S. economy (GDP [gross domestic product]), consumers, and industry, including impact on domestic natural gas prices; (v) job creation; (vi) U.S. balance of trade; (vii) international considerations; and (viii) environmental considerations. DOE reiterated, however, that the listed criteria "are not exclusive" and that "other issues" may be considered.

To date, DOE has granted one long-term application to export domestically produced LNG to non-FTA countries— for Sabine Pass Liquefaction, LLC, in 2011. Sixteen other natural gas export license applications, dating back to 2010, remain pending. After the Sabine Pass approval, DOE undertook a two-part study to evaluate the cumulative economic impact of LNG exports. The Energy Information Administration (EIA) conducted the first part of the study, which examined the potential impact of additional natural gas exports on domestic energy consumption, production, and prices under several export scenarios. The second part of the study, conducted by the private economic consulting firm NERA [National Economic Research Associates] and originally due before the November 2012 election, was issued on December 5, 2012. The NERA report assessed the potential macroeconomic impact of LNG exports. Neither the EIA report nor the NERA report examines the national security implications of potential gas export transactions.

Both reports have been placed in all 16 pending export license dockets. The DOE solicited, and has received, initial public comments on the study. Reply comments are due by February 25, 2013. The agency stated that it will only begin to make final decisions regarding the pending export applications when it has evaluated both the study and all comments. At that time, applications will be evaluated in the order of priority announced by DOE earlier this year.

The federal government regulates exports of domestically produced crude oil pursuant to the Energy Policy and Conservation Act of 1975, which instituted an export licensing system intended to address "short supply" conditions in the United States. Under the current system, all U.S. exports of crude oil require a license from the Bureau of Industry and Security (BIS), an agency within the Department of Commerce [DOC].

The approval of crude oil export license applications by BIS will depend on whether the transaction meets certain listed criteria. According to the Export Administration Regulations (EAR) on short-supply controls, approval standards are divided among two categories of crude oil exports: (i) presumption of approval, and (ii) approval only in the "national interest." For the first category, BIS will approve export applications that satisfy one of several discrete conditions, including "exports to Canada for consumption or use therein."

For the second category, BIS will review applications on a case-by-case basis and "generally will approve such applications if BIS determines that the proposed export is consistent with the national interest and the purposes of the Energy Policy and Conservation Act [EPCA]." The agency retains discretion to approve or reject these applications, although the EAR notes that two types of exports "will be among those that BIS will determine to be in the national interest and consistent with the purposes of EPCA": (i) those with equivalent crude oil or other petroleum product imports, made under contracts that may be terminated if U.S. petroleum supplies are interrupted or seriously threatened, and where the applicant can demonstrate that, for compelling economic or technological reasons beyond his control, the crude oil "cannot reasonably be marketed in the United States"; or (ii) those involving temporary exports or exchanges that are consistent with various statutory exceptions.

According to an April 2012 Congressional Research Service report, few crude oil export license applications have been granted under the "national interest" exception, and none since 2000. The *Financial Times* reported in October 2012 that six companies have applied for export licenses for shipments to Canada and other countries. The BIS has not yet announced its decision on these applications, and the proceedings are confidential. Thus, similar to the export licensing system for natural gas, BIS has discretion to consider license applications for most crude oil exports under the "national interest" rule, and several pending applications have been delayed for months.

Policy Concerns Raised by the Current Licensing Systems

U.S. export licensing restrictions on natural gas and crude oil raise significant economic, legal and political concerns.

The current export restrictions create a host of economic problems. First, by depressing domestic prices and subjecting export approval to government discretion, the U.S. licensing systems retard domestic energy production, discourage investment in the oil and gas sectors, and destabilize the domestic energy market. Artificially low prices prevent producers from achieving a sustainable rate of return on the massive up-front costs required to drill and extract oil and gas, and investors lack any assurances under the discretionary licensing systems that domestic prices will not collapse when output increases. In fact, recent low domestic gas prices caused many U.S. energy companies to sell assets and shutter new projects. These same concerns affect the domestic crude oil market and have led the IEA to warn that the current export restrictions have put the "American oil boom" at risk.

According to the EIA report commissioned by DOE, increased natural gas exports would lead to higher prices followed by increased domestic production. But prices are not expected to skyrocket, and consumers will continue to benefit from hypercompetitive fuel and feedstock supplies. Independent reports from the Brookings Institution and Deloitte [Touche Tohmatsu Limited] project that permitting gas exports would lead to a small and gradual increase in domestic natural gas prices. Such predictability and consistency is good for the industry and the overall stability of the U.S. energy market—it would prevent boom and bust cycles of high/low prices and high/low production that hurt the U.S. economy and prevent companies from implementing long-term investment, production, and hiring strategies. The current situation—in which oil and gas export decisions are left to the whims of federal regulators—has the opposite effect.

Second, restricting U.S. gas and oil exports could hurt the U.S. economy. Recent studies indicate that U.S. natural gas producers could earn up to $3 billion per year from exports. The Sabine Pass liquefaction facility—the lone DOE approval, thus far—is projected to create 30,000 to 50,000 new American jobs.

The export benefits would not be limited to energy producers, however. The NERA report found that LNG exports, even in unlimited quantities, would produce gains in real household income.

Beyond the economic problems, both export licensing systems raise serious concerns under global trade rules. First, the U.S. export licensing regimes for natural gas and crude oil likely violate U.S. obligations under the General Agreement on Tariffs and Trade (GATT). Under GATT Article XI:1, WTO [World Trade Organization] members are generally prohibited from imposing quantitative restrictions on imports and exports. Under Article XI and related WTO jurisprudence, "discretionary" licensing systems (i.e., those in which the administering authority has the freedom to grant or deny a license) and systems in which applications are delayed for several months constitute impermissible restrictions on export quantities. On the other hand, licensing systems in which approval is automatic and relatively quick (e.g., five days) have been found to be lawful.

Based on these standards, both the U.S. natural gas and crude oil licensing systems appear to violate GATT Article XI:1. Each system provides the administering agency (DOE or BIS) with the discretion to grant or deny an export license based on subjective and nonbinding criteria (the "public interest" or "national interest" standards). Moreover, the pending export license applications have been delayed for several months (and, in a few cases, years). Both of these facts support findings of GATT violations.

One or both licensing systems might theoretically be defended under the national security exception of GATT Article XXI, which permits members to impose WTO-inconsistent measures "which it considers necessary for the protection of its essential security interests . . . taken in time of . . . emergency in international relations." No panel has ever ruled on the national security exception, but the standard is subjective: the text refers to a measure which the WTO member considers "essential" for its security interests. Thus, a WTO panel might defer to a member's definition of what constitutes an "essential" security interest.

Given that crude oil exports are regulated under the same apparatus, and by the same agency (BIS), as other goods regulated for express national security purposes, the U.S. government might be able to successfully invoke GATT Article XXI to defend the system from allegations of WTO inconsistency. However, it is unclear whether the U.S. government would want to establish international legal precedent on "essential" security measures for a relatively obscure export restriction that has been in place since 1975 (i.e., during periods that were arguably not times of "emergency in international relations").

The Current Gas Export Policy Is Contrary to U.S. Objective

These same limitations could apply to the 1930s-origin natural gas licensing system, as could several others. For example, the laws that govern the export of products that could have national security concerns do not appear to apply to natural gas. Gas exports are regulated by DOE, rather than BIS (which, as noted above, typically handles national security–related export controls). Finally, economic, not security, issues appear to drive the "public interest" standard and DOE's application of it. Only one of the public-interest criteria (U.S. "energy security") could be considered to relate to national security, but the available legislative history of the original 1938 act and the subsequent amendments do not indicate that the export licensing system was implemented for national security purposes. Also, both the reports informing DOE's decisions on the pending LNG export applications address only economic matters. Thus, the U.S. government could be even more hesitant to claim that the natural gas system is "essential" to the country's national security.

Second, restrictive export licensing systems also raise potential concerns under global anti-subsidy disciplines. There is limited WTO jurisprudence on whether an "export restraint" that lowers domestic input prices for downstream manufacturers constitutes a "subsidy" as defined by the WTO Agreement on Subsidies and Countervailing Measures. The WTO panel in *U.S.—Export Restraints* [formally known as *United States—Measures Treating Export Restraints as Subsidies*] found that certain export measures did not meet the WTO's precise definition. However, the panel's ruling was specific to the measures at issue and was not appealed to the WTO appellate body, whose rulings have more precedential value. No other disputes have addressed this issue.

Moreover, the panel ruling has not stopped national governments from imposing anti-subsidy measures (called "countervailing duties" or "CVDs") on downstream exports due to export restrictions on various upstream inputs. Most notably, the Department of Commerce has stated repeatedly that export restrictions are a type of "indirect subsidy." And DOC continues to treat them as such in new CVD investigations. Furthermore, the European Commission in January 2013 recommended the imposition of anti-subsidy duties on Chinese exports of organic coated steel, finding that the Chinese government provided the subsidies "mainly through export restrictions that artificially lower prices of rolled steel for domestic manufacturers."

Thus, the crude oil and natural gas licensing systems might not only raise legal problems for the U.S. government, but could subject certain energy-intensive U.S exporters to anti-subsidy duties that negate the competitive price advantages created by the licensing systems.

Current policy is also at odds with other Obama administration policies. First, the restrictive export licensing systems undermine the National Export Initiative (NEI) and its goal of doubling U.S. exports between 2009 and 2014. Second, the administration's reticence with respect to fossil fuel exports stands in stark contrast to its full-throated advocacy of other energy exports, particularly renewables like biofuels and solar panels. Indeed, the September 2010 White House report setting forth the NEI's priority recommendations calls for increased government support for renewable and nuclear energy exports—but never mentions oil or natural gas. A November 2012 follow-up report lauds the U.S. government's efforts to achieve these objectives, yet continues to ignore American fossil fuels, despite the massive increases in production and export potential that occurred between 2010 and 2012. Furthermore, increased fossil fuel exports could actually spur domestic production of renewable energy through higher oil and gas prices. According to the EIA, the role of renewables in electricity generation would be "greater in a higher-gas-price environment."

Third, the use of export restrictions to benefit downstream industries contradicts long-standing U.S. policy with respect to export restraints and illegal subsidies. The Commerce Department repeatedly has imposed anti-subsidy duties on imports due to countervail subsidies resulting from foreign export restrictions on upstream inputs. The administration's embrace of similar restrictions would not only be hypocritical, but would also expose U.S. exports of energy-intensive products (e.g., fertilizer) to "copycat" duties in key foreign markets.

Fourth, the U.S. government has long opposed restrictive and opaque export licensing systems in WTO negotiations and dispute settlement. For example, in *China—Raw Materials* [formally known as *China—Measures Related to the Exportation of Various Raw Materials*], the U.S. government challenged China's "non-automatic" export licensing systems for various raw materials as impermissible restrictions on exportation in violation of GATT Article XI. In March 2009, the United States and several other countries submitted a proposal to the WTO negotiating group on market access calling for increased disciplines on members' use of export licensing. The current U.S. export licensing regulations for oil and gas contradict these positions and undermine laudable efforts to rein in such restrictions globally.

Steps Needed to Improve Energy Trade Policy

If the president really wants to develop America's vast energy resources, grow the U.S. economy, restore some coherence to U.S. trade and energy policy, and avoid potentially embarrassing trade conflicts, he should order the immediate approval of all pending license applications and then pursue, with Congress, an overhaul of our archaic licensing systems. Specifically, the White House and Congress should take the following steps to improve and modernize U.S. energy trade policy:

- First, DOE and BIS should immediately approve the pending export-license applications for natural gas and crude oil, and approve all future applications on a transparent, expedited basis. Such actions would bolster investment, production, and employment in the oil and gas sector, benefit the overall U.S. economy, avoid the myriad policy and legal problems raised by the current system, and gain a rare moment of bipartisan praise from Congress and the general public. Although some people question whether natural gas exports will benefit the U.S. economy in the long term, clearly the people best situated to make that determination are those risking billions of dollars of their own money, not heavily lobbied government officials in Washington, D.C. Moreover, rejecting or delaying the pending applications could further undermine public support for our political system, as the government would likely be seen as subsidizing certain politically connected producers or coddling environmentalists at the expense of upstream energy producers, their workers, and the U.S. economy more broadly.

- Second, the White House should work with Congress this year to consolidate and overhaul the U.S. export licensing regime for energy products. All energy exports—fossil fuels, renewables, nuclear, etc.—should be regulated by a single agency and subject to a transparent licensing system whereby applications are automatically approved within a finite period, unless the agency can demonstrate a tangible and immediate national security risk. These changes would create a more stable and secure domestic energy market and get the federal government out of the business of picking winners and losers therein. They also would conform U.S. trade policy to today's energy and economic realities and to global trade and subsidy rules.

Periodical and Internet Sources Bibliography

The following articles have been selected to supplement the diverse views presented in this chapter.

James Bacchus	"U.S. Should Rethink Restrictions on Natural Gas Exports," *International Business Times*, August 19, 2013.
Doug Bandow	"Free America's Energy Future: Drop Washington's Counterproductive Oil and Natural Gas Export Ban," *Forbes*, January 27, 2014.
Matthew Daly	"Plans to Export US Natural Gas Stir Debate," Associated Press, May 12, 2013.
Michael Economides	"Hands Off: Why the Free Market Should Control the Valve to US Natural Gas Exports," *Energy Tribune*, February 27, 2013.
Amy Harder	"Approval of Natural-Gas Export Project Gets Mixed Reaction from Lawmakers," *Wall Street Journal*, March 24, 2014.
Wendy Koch	"U.S. Natural Gas Exports Poised for Takeoff Despite Debate," *USA Today*, April 7, 2014.
Clifford Krauss and Nelson D. Schwartz	"Foreseeing Trouble in Exporting Natural Gas," *New York Times*, August 15, 2013.
Kiley Kroh	"Why Exporting Natural Gas Isn't a Simple Solution to the Russia Problem," *ClimateProgress*, March 28, 2014.
Bill McKibben and Mike Tidwell	"A Big Fracking Lie," *Politico Magazine*, January 21, 2014.
Pete Olson	"Exporting Natural Gas Will Help US Economy," *The Hill*, April 14, 2014.

OPPOSING
VIEWPOINTS®
SERIES

CHAPTER 4

Should Offshore Drilling for Gas Be Permitted?

Chapter Preface

Competition for natural resources has been a reason for many territorial claims and conflicts throughout history. The South China Sea region—with its vast supplies of natural gas and oil reserves—has become a potential hot spot as bordering countries stake out their claims to the area. For decades, the countries bordering the South China Sea have had competing territorial and jurisdictional claims over this part of the Pacific Ocean. Among the countries laying claim to all or part of this territory are China, Vietnam, the Philippines, Malaysia, Brunei, Taiwan, and Indonesia. With the discovery of oil and gas reserves below the ocean floor of the South China Sea and the development of deepwater drilling technologies in the late 1970s, the competition for this region escalated. Explorations have determined that there are at least eleven billion barrels of oil and 190 trillion cubic feet of natural gas as yet untapped.

Seeking to become less dependent on oil from the Middle East, several countries asserted claims to this area, according to Patrick Barta and Cris Larano in an August 3, 2011, article in the *Wall Street Journal*:

> Advances in oil and gas exploration, along with stubbornly high energy prices, are adding to the stress. Improved deepwater-drilling technology is making it easier for oil companies to prospect in far-out areas of the sea that used to be out of reach, increasing the strategic importance of controlling as much of it as possible. Meanwhile, with oil prices hovering around $95 a barrel and energy demand outpacing new supply in Asia, the urgency to step up exploration is intensifying, leading to more conflicts.

As tensions have risen in the area, some observers see the potential for conflict. According to Bonnie S. Glaser, senior fellow at the Center for Strategic and International Studies,

"Disputes between China and Vietnam over seismic surveys or drilling for oil and gas could ... trigger an armed clash. ... China has harassed PetroVietnam oil survey ships in the past that were searching for oil and gas deposits in Vietnam's EEZ [exclusive economic zone]."

On the other side of the debate, Nicolas Jenny says in a March 18, 2014, article in *International Policy Digest* that even if oil and gas deposits exist, they would prove too expensive to extract. He explains, "The cost of drilling a deepwater well is around $30 to $60 million, or about five times more than drilling in shallow waters. And while the cost might not put all investors off, the risk of being mired in a political dispute will."

Along with political issues, there are economic and environmental concerns regarding drilling offshore for natural gas. In the following chapter, scientists, commentators, and journalists debate these issues.

> *"It is a widely overlooked fact that natural hydrocarbon seeps generally have a larger impact on the marine environment than do oil and gas exploration and production."*

Offshore Gas Drilling Benefits the Economy and the Environment

Bruce Allen

Bruce Allen is cofounder of Stop Oil Seeps (SOS) California, an environmental nonprofit organization based in Santa Barbara, California. In the following viewpoint, Allen claims that environmentalists who oppose offshore drilling for gas and oil ignore the fact that offshore drilling has actually resulted in a reduction in hydrocarbon pollution. He makes the point that the largest source of marine hydrocarbon pollution comes from natural oil seepage. Drilling for gas and oil lowers the amount of natural oil seepage, thus reducing environmental damage while also creating economic benefits, Allen contends.

As you read, consider the following questions:

1. According to the National Academy of Sciences, what percentage of hydrocarbon pollution in US waters is due to natural seeps, and what percentage is due to offshore drilling?

2. What are some of the environmental impacts of the offshore Santa Barbara oil seepage zone?

3. What are some of the benefits of the modern slant and horizontal drilling that have occurred off the California coast, according to the author?

The oceans surrounding the United States hold tremendous oil and natural gas potential, but much of that potential is not being realized. Nearly 85 percent of these waters—the Atlantic, the Pacific, and the eastern Gulf of Mexico—are off-limits to exploration and drilling. Government studies estimate that these restricted areas hold at least 19 billion barrels of oil—nearly 30 years' worth of current imports from Saudi Arabia—and oil estimates are known to increase as exploration occurs. The greatest untapped potential lies in the Pacific. Producing this oil would increase oil supplies, lower prices, and generate large tax revenues—while creating thousands of jobs in the domestic energy industry.

Drilling restrictions in general are imposed due to environmental concerns, despite the fact that offshore environmental damage has been greatly reduced by technologies that minimize the risk of oil spills and other hazards to the environment. In fact, offshore oil production has *lowered* the amount of oil released into the ocean by reducing natural seepage of oil, especially in areas with active offshore oil seeps, such as California's Santa Barbara coast.

Natural hydrocarbon seeps have historically been used to locate the world's usable sources of oil and tar. Papers published by British Petroleum [presently known as BP] in the early 1990s show that over 75 percent of the world's oil basins contain surface oil seeps. Most seeps emit small volumes of oil and gas that do not significantly deplete hydrocarbon reservoirs over the short term, but can add up to significant depletion of oil and gas over the longer term.

The knowledge that surface seepage has a direct link to subsurface oil and gas accumulations is not new and has been the impetus for many of the world's early major oil and gas discoveries by pioneers of oil production—as far back as ancient China, and more recently the 1860s in Pennsylvania and the 1890s in Azerbaijan. Natural seeps were the impetus for early exploration of oil in Iran and Iraq in the early 1900s.

Natural hydrocarbon seeps continue to be an important indicator of economic oil and gas resources. The high cost of deepwater offshore oil and gas exploration has made the identification of hydrocarbon seeps an important consideration in oil-exploration risk-reduction methods.

Natural Seeps: The Largest Source of U.S. Marine Hydrocarbon Pollution

Natural hydrocarbon seeps generally result from pressurized hydrocarbon reservoirs that force oil and gas up through fissures to the earth's surface either on land or the seabed floor where the hydrocarbons escape in the form of oil, tar, and methane-rich gases.

It is a widely overlooked fact that natural hydrocarbon seeps generally have a larger impact on the marine environment than do oil and gas exploration and production. According to the National Academy of Sciences, 63 percent of hydrocarbon pollution in U.S. waters stems from natural seeps, while only 1 percent is due to offshore drilling and extraction. Geologists believe that over the course of millions of years, more oil has seeped naturally into the earth's environment than currently exists in all conventional oil reservoirs combined.

The Gulf of Mexico, for instance, is a major U.S. offshore oil- and gas-producing region where the environmental impact of natural hydrocarbon seepage appears to far exceed the environmental impact of accidental oil releases due to commercial extraction and transportation.

Onshore hydrocarbon seeps are also pervasive in many areas of the world, and are a source of contamination for many streambeds and rivers. The Santa Susana Mountains in California are estimated to contain 22,000 active oil seeps that are associated with significant streambed contamination.

One of the most studied offshore oil and gas seep regions over the last 40 years is the Santa Barbara coast of California, which has the world's second most prolific oil seepage areas, extending for about 80 miles along the coastline. The offshore Santa Barbara oil seepage zones result in about 70,000 barrels per year of oil and tar seepage into the Pacific, much of which washes up on California beaches. Every four years, the amount of offshore Santa Barbara oil seepage exceeds the 240,000 barrels that spilled from the *Exxon Valdez* in 1989. . . . Far more birds and wildlife have been killed in the last 40 years by California's offshore oil seepage than by all previous California offshore oil production spills combined, including the 1969 spill [in which eighty thousand to one hundred thousand barrels of crude oil spilled into the Santa Barbara channel].

Seeps are also one of the world's largest methane gas emission sources, and are a major source of air pollution in Santa Barbara County. These coastal California seeps release oil and tar that washes ashore along nearly half the coastline of California, with the highest concentrations in Santa Barbara County. In the winter, the Davidson Current washes seep oil and tar ashore as far north as the beaches of Santa Cruz and San Francisco.

The California Department of Fish [and Wildlife] often receives public calls reporting a possible oil spill on California central coast beaches, which is invariably determined to be natural seepage. The California Department of Fish [and Wild-life] requires that seep oil and tar collected on California beaches be treated as hazardous waste, the same as for industrial oil spills.

Offshore Production: Significant Reductions in Oil Pollution on California Beaches

One of the side effects of offshore oil production has been the reduction of oil and gas seepage due to decreases in subsea oil-reservoir pressure. Seep oil is chemically the same as commercially extracted oil, although the seep oil and tar have often undergone partial oxidation by the time they move into the water or onshore.

The seepage reductions due to offshore oil and gas extraction have, in some cases, resulted in significant reductions in natural oil and gas seep pollution over the last 40 years.

There are also anecdotal observations and research indicating that oil production around the world is responsible for ongoing reductions in hydrocarbon seepage pollution.

Ironically, the decreased oil and gas reservoir pressure due to ongoing "legacy" offshore oil and gas production (which continued even after the state-wide offshore moratorium was imposed) near the site of the famous 1969 Santa Barbara oil spill is resulting in reductions in California's coastal seepage pollution. California beaches have become significantly cleaner over the last 50 years due to offshore oil and gas production.

Modern slant and horizontal drilling is extending these benefits into seep zones located further into the ocean than the areas immediately surrounding existing offshore production platforms. Central and southern California beaches have been polluted by this natural seep oil for well over 100,000 years. A 22-year study of the offshore oil platform Holly off the Californian coast concluded that, "Oil production here has resulted in an unexpected benefit to the atmosphere and marine environment." According to peer-reviewed University of

California research, if offshore production were expanded in the seep zone areas studied, there would be further reductions in seepage pollution and the associated methane gas and ozone-forming reactive organic compounds (ROCs).

Longtime Santa Barbara residents have also observed for the last 50 years that their beaches have seen significant reductions in seepage oil and tar beach pollution. The simple fact is that California offshore oil and gas production has been the reason why California's prolific natural oil and gas seepage pollution has been declining for decades. California beaches are becoming cleaner thanks to existing legacy offshore oil and gas production. Geologists believe these reductions in seepage pollution will last for thousands of years.

Offshore hydrocarbon seeps are also a naturally dynamic process. In addition to reduced seepage due to reservoir pressure reductions from commercial extraction, seeps can also become active in new areas due to earthquakes and other natural events. In 2007, an earthquake in New Zealand resulted in a new offshore seepage area that led to exploration activity to determine the underlying reservoir's production potential. This seep zone off the New Zealand coast had previously not been explored for the presence of economically recoverable hydrocarbons.

In Santa Barbara, a 6.8 magnitude earthquake in 1925 resulted in a large spontaneous release of undersea reservoir oil off the coast that boiled up from the seafloor and inundated the coastline and beaches with extensive oil slicks. The Southern California 1971 Sylmar earthquake also resulted in new offshore seep areas observed in previously unrecorded areas.

In January 2005, an increase in natural seepage off the California coast resulted in oil slicks that covered more than 20 square miles. The increased seepage subsided over the following weeks.

Since Californian offshore production began in the late 1950s, far more wildlife has been killed (using bird death estimates as a surrogate) by California's offshore natural oil seeps than by all of California offshore oil production spills combined. It is an interesting artifact of the offshore oil debate that large numbers of bird deaths due to natural oil seepage garner no media attention, whereas small numbers of bird deaths due to a small oil spill cause extensive national attention and outrage by opponents of offshore oil production— even in areas where offshore production has been consistently reducing pollution caused by natural seepage.

A new study estimates that oil seepage off the Santa Barbara coast from one seep area alone (Coal Oil Point) has resulted in current oil sediment deposits between 8 and 80 times the amount of oil released from the *Exxon Valdez* spill.

There are also concerns about air pollution resulting from seepage. Gas emissions from hydrocarbon seeps are estimated to be one of the largest sources of methane released annually into the earth's atmosphere, and studies indicate that existing oil and gas production may be causing ongoing reductions in methane emissions worldwide. Methane is a potent greenhouse gas. Natural offshore seep emissions are one of the largest sources of air pollution in Santa Barbara County.

Oil Seeps: Indicators of Oil and Gas Reserves

The presence of natural oil seeps has led to the discovery of some of the world's largest oil fields. The second-largest oil field ever discovered, the Cantarell "supergiant" field, was discovered after a fisherman, Rudesindo Cantarell [Jiménez], repeatedly complained to the Mexican national oil company PEMEX [Petróleos Mexicanos] that his fishing nets were being covered with oil in the Gulf of Mexico. PEMEX had no oil operations in Mr. Cantarell's fishing area. The company investigated the source of the offshore oil and subsequently discovered an offshore oil field in 1976 which had produced more than 12 billion barrels of oil by 2007. Although being depleted rapidly, the Cantarell field is still one of Mexico's largest single sources of oil production.

At current rates of oil seepage off the Santa Barbara coast, about 7 billion barrels of oil may already have seeped into the California coastal marine environment over the last 100,000 years. The life span of the Santa Barbara offshore oil seeps is estimated to exceed 400,000 years. Seven billion barrels of oil represents approximately 25 percent of all current U.S. oil reserves. Seven billion barrels of new Santa Barbara offshore oil production would supply all of California's current imported oil needs for the next 25 years.

National Offshore Energy Policy Should Consider Natural Oil and Gas Seepage

Natural oil and gas seeps are by far the largest sources of hydrocarbon pollution released into U.S. coastal waters and are a major source of offshore oil pollution and atmospheric methane emissions worldwide. Oil and gas seeps are also one of the most important indicators for locating recoverable hydrocarbon resources. California's central and south coast has seen significant environmental benefits from the reductions in coastal seepage pollution due to offshore oil and gas production. California's coastal environment would benefit from offshore oil and gas expansion in active seep areas that are currently off-limits in California waters, as well as in federal seep zone waters in the Santa Maria basin in the Outer Continental Shelf. Thus offshore oil and gas production represents both an effective means of addressing the problems of seepage pollution as well as an economic opportunity.

Continued research may also show that the long-term environmental benefits that coastal California has experienced due to offshore oil and gas extraction may be occurring in other regions as well—albeit probably to a lesser degree.

The economic benefits from increased domestic hydrocarbon production are well known, but many erroneously assume they come at an environmental cost. In truth, there are opportunities, off Santa Barbara and elsewhere, to achieve substantial environmental benefits from drilling as a consequence of reduced seepage of oil and natural gas into the air and water. Expanded offshore oil and gas production can genuinely be a win-win proposition.

"Fracking is an inherently dangerous practice that has no place in our fragile coastal ecosystem."

Offshore Gas Drilling Harms the Environment

Emily Jeffers

Emily Jeffers is staff attorney for the oceans program at the Center for Biological Diversity. In a letter to the California Coastal Commission, Jeffers urges the commissioners to immediately halt fracking for oil and gas off the California coast because of potential harm to marine life and the coastal environment. Offshore fracking increases risks to water quality, increases air pollution, increases vessel traffic, causes light pollution, and has the potential to induce earthquakes, Jeffers contends. She says it is the responsibility of the California Coastal Commission to protect marine life and the environment, and therefore the commission must either ban fracking or properly regulate it.

As you read, consider the following questions:

1. Why is water contamination a particular hazard with offshore fracking, according to the author?

Emily Jeffers, "Re: The Coastal Commission's Regulatory Authority and Mandates Relating to Fracking in Oil and Gas Wells Offshore California," Center for Biological Diversity, November 14, 2013.

2. How does offshore fracking contribute to air pollution, according to the author?

3. What evidence does the author use to support her claim that fracking induces earthquakes?

The Center for Biological Diversity urges the California Coastal Commission to take immediate action to halt hydraulic fracturing (fracking) and other unconventional techniques for extracting oil and gas off the California coast. . . .

Fracking is an inherently dangerous practice that has no place in our fragile coastal ecosystem. It increases the environmental damages and risks beyond those of conventional oil development and poses a threat of serious harm to marine life and the coastal environment. The commission must use its broad delegation of authority under the California Coastal Act to protect wildlife, marine fisheries, and the natural environment from the practice. Because the risk of many of the harms from fracking cannot be eliminated, a complete prohibition on fracking is the best way to protect human health and the environment.

Absent a total ban, the coastal commission can take several concrete, proactive steps under the Coastal Act to limit the practice in state and federal waters and ensure the continued health of our coastal ecosystem. . . .

Environmental Risks and Damages from Fracking

Offshore fracking directly and negatively impacts the coastal resources the coastal commission is charged with preserving. By allowing fracking to occur in this "delicately balanced ecosystem," the coastal commission is abrogating its duty to protect wildlife, marine fisheries, and the ecological balance of the coastal zone. On land, fracking, drilling, and the resulting toxic wastewater have developed an extensive track record of spills, accidents, leaks, pollution, and property damage; offshore, those effects are heightened by the added complications of operating in a difficult environment. The damages from fracking and drilling to air, water, wildlife, and health have been severe, and often irreversible. Yet the full extent of the risks and the long-term impacts are not even yet fully understood. Hundreds of carcinogenic and toxic chemicals are known to be used in fracking, but the full extent and composition of chemicals used in fracking is undisclosed by industry. The latest fracking techniques, including the high-volume, high-pressure use of the chemical fracking fluid combined with horizontal drilling, have been in use for only about a decade, yet in that time have transformed the oil and gas industry and led to drilling booms around the country by facilitating production from shale formations that could not previously be economically developed. The environmental and community destruction have been dramatic. This experience with onshore fracking, along with the additional factors discussed in detail below, demonstrates the serious threat fracking poses to the coastal environment when conducted in our oceans.

Fracking Uses Toxic Chemicals and Increases Risks to Water Quality

The coastal commission is charged with protecting the "quality of coastal waters . . . appropriate to maintain optimum populations of marine organisms and for the protection of human health." This is achieved through, among other means, "minimizing adverse effects of wastewater discharges." Currently the coastal commission is failing to achieve this mandate because uncontrolled fracking is occurring off the California coast.

While industry claims that companies have been safely fracking wells in California for decades, modern fracking is new, different, and more perilous. Today, to help profitably draw oil out of shale formations, companies will drill exten-

In the offshore context, fracking fluid is either discharged into the ocean or transported for onshore underground injection. When disposed of at sea, these chemicals enter the marine ecosystem. The coastal commission acknowledges that approximately half of the platforms in the Santa Barbara Channel discharge all or a portion of their wastewater directly to the ocean. This produced wastewater contains all of the chemicals injected originally into the fracked wells, with the addition of toxins gathered from the subsurface environment. These discharges of toxic chemicals directly contravene the requirements of the Coastal Act, which charges the coastal commission with the "protection against the spillage of . . . hazardous substances."

While the impacts to wildlife have received little study, these chemicals clearly pose a threat to marine life. Toxic chemicals that enter the marine environment will impact marine life and sensitive habitats. California has many species of whales, porpoises, dolphins, pinnipeds, and sea otters. More than 500 species of fish live off the shores of Southern California. The coastal waters off California are a productive foraging region for whales and sea turtles and support a myriad of wildlife. . . .

Fracking Increases Air Pollution

The coastal commission has a duty to protect the coastal environment, including air pollution resulting from the operation of oil and gas facilities in the coastal zone. . . . The Coastal Act also requires that marine resources and biological productivity in coastal waters be maintained and restored, which includes protecting animals, such as whales and sea turtles, from inhaling dangerous air pollutants.

Oil and gas operations emit numerous air pollutants, including volatile organic compounds ("VOCs"), nitrogen oxides ("NOx"), non-methane hydrocarbons ("NMHCs"), particulate matter ("PM"), hydrogen sulfide, and methane. VOC emissions, which make up about 3.5 percent of the gases emitted by oil or gas operations, are particularly hazardous. VOC emissions include the BTEX compounds—benzene, toluene, ethyl benzene, and xylene—which are hazardous air pollutants. Health effects associated with benzene include "acute and chronic nonlymphocytic leukemia, acute myeloid leukemia, chronic lymphocytic leukemia, anemia, and other blood disorders and immunological effects." Further, maternal exposure to benzene has been associated with an increase in birth prevalence of neural tube defects. Xylene exposure also can cause eye, nose, and throat irritation, difficulty in breathing, impaired lung function, and nervous system impairment. In fact, many of the volatile chemicals associated with drilling and oil and gas waste are associated with serious effects to the respiratory, nervous, or circulatory system. Also, a recent study sampling air quality near Colorado gas wells found additional cause for concern regarding VOC emissions: among other things, it found methylene chloride in high concentrations. The study states that for the wells tested "[m]ethylene chloride, a toxic solvent not reported in products used in drilling or fracking, was detected 73% of the time; several times in high concentrations," including one reading of 1730 ppbv [parts per billion by volume]. While the source of the methylene chloride was not entirely clear, the study reported that it is stored on well pads for cleaning purposes. . . .

Oil and gas operations release large amounts of methane. Natural gas emissions are generally about 84 percent methane. While the exact amount is not clear, EPA [Environmental Protection Agency] has estimated that "oil and gas systems are the largest human-made source of methane emissions and account for 37 percent of methane emissions in the United States or 3.8 percent of the total greenhouse gas emissions in the United States." Methane leakage is a problem in Southern California. A recent study of methane emissions in the Los

Angeles basin found that a startling 17 percent of total methane produced was leaked or vented to the atmosphere.

Emissions of methane, one of the most potent greenhouse gases, are of great concern because they contribute significantly to climate change. Methane's global warming potential is approximately 33 times that of carbon dioxide over a 100-year time frame and 105 times that of carbon dioxide over a 20-year time frame. Oil and gas development contributes to greenhouse gas emissions from the operations, refining, and end use of the extracted oil or gas. Fracking increases these emissions because it extends the life of a well, and may facilitate oil development that is otherwise uneconomical. . . .

Offshore Fracking Will Increase Vessel Traffic and Light Pollution

The activities associated with fracking and the prolonged lifetime of oil and gas platforms as a result of new unconventional oil extraction methods will result in increases in vessel traffic and light pollution that in turn have adverse impacts on marine mammals and seabirds, respectively.

Offshore fracking is likely to increase vessel traffic and its associated impacts because vessels will be needed to service the wells, transport fracking fluids and sands, and dispose of wastes generated during the process. It may also increase vessel traffic as a result of extending the life of oil and gas operations and increasing interest in oil development in Pacific waters. Vessel traffic increases noise pollution that may interfere with important biological functions of marine mammals like feeding, mating, and rearing young. The number of whales killed by collisions with commercial vessels has climbed within recent years to unsustainable levels. Ambient ocean noise from ship traffic continues to raise the din against which marine animals must struggle to carry out normal life.

Ship strike-related mortality is a documented threat to endangered Pacific coast populations of fin, humpback, blue,

Exposure to Gas Drilling Kills Cattle

A beef cattle farmer had a herd of 96 cattle (Angus-Limousin cross) that was divided among three pastures. The farm is located in an area of intensive gas drilling, with two active shallow vertical gas wells on the farmer's property and approximately 190 active gas wells within five miles of the property; of these, approximately 11 are shale gas wells and approximately 26 are deep vertical gas wells. In one pasture, 60 cows (a mixed herd, mostly 5- to 10-year-old bred cows) had access to a creek as a source of water. In a second pasture, 20 cows (bred yearlings) obtained water from hillside runoff, and in a third pasture, 14 feeder calves (8 to 14 months old) and two bulls had access to a pond. Over a three-month period, 21 head from the creek-side pasture died (17 adult bred cows and 4 calves). All the cattle were healthy before this episode. Despite symptomatic treatment, deaths occurred 1 to 3 days after the cows went down and were unable to rise. Basic diagnostics were done, but no cause of death was determined.... Of the 39 cows on the creek-side pasture that survived, 16 failed to breed and several cows produced stillborn calves with white and blue eyes. The health of the cattle on the other two pastures was unaffected; on the second pasture, only one cow failed to breed. Historically, the health of the herd was good, the farmer reporting average losses of 1–2 cows a year in his herd of nearly 100 cattle.

Michelle Bamberger and Robert E. Oswald,
"Impacts of Gas Drilling on Human and Animal Health,"
Scientific Solutions, *2012.*

sperm, and killer whales. Ship strikes are an increasing problem in California. Between 2001 and 2010, nearly 50 large whales off the California coast were documented as having been struck by ships. The Santa Barbara Channel is an important blue whale habitat. Between June and November, high densities of endangered blue whales spend time feeding on the abundant planktonic krill in the area of these oil and gas activities. In fact, blue whales have developed a particular affinity for the area such that the Santa Barbara Channel hosts the world's densest summer seasonal congregation of blues. Another endangered whale, the humpback whale, congregates in the area from May to September. Little is known about the elusive endangered fin whales; however, congregations have been observed near feeding aggravations of blue and humpback whales. Although rare, endangered sperm, right, and killer whales occasionally occur in the area. Gray whales migrate through the region in the late fall on their way south to breeding grounds and again in the late winter and early spring on their way north to feeding areas, and minke whales are known to occupy the region year-round. Increased oil and gas activities will interfere with important habitat and increase the risks of ship strikes.

Fracking extends the life of offshore oil and gas platforms with associated impacts from lighting to wildlife. Seabirds are vulnerable to disorientation from oil and gas operations that increase light pollution. Artificial lighting from the proposed action must be more fully evaluated. Artificial light attracts seabirds at night, especially nocturnally active species such as auks, shearwaters, and storm petrels, and disrupts their normal foraging and breeding activities in several ways. In a phenomenon called light entrapment, seabirds continually circle lights and flares on vessels and energy platforms, instead of foraging or visiting their nests, which can lead to exhaustion and mortality. Seabirds also frequently collide with lights or structures around lights, causing injury or mortality, or strand on lighted platforms where they are vulnerable to injury, oiling or other feather contamination, and exhaustion.

Fracking and the Disposal of Fracking Wastewater Can Induce Earthquakes

Any development in the coastal zone must "neither create nor contribute significantly to geologic instability." Scientists have long known that oil and gas activities are capable of triggering earthquakes, with records of the connection going back to the 1920s. In California, oil and gas extraction has in the past likely induced strong earthquakes, including two over 6.0 in magnitude. Recent studies have also drawn a strong connection between the recent rise in wastewater injection and increased earthquake rates. Wastewater injection has likely been triggering seismic events in Arkansas, Colorado, Ohio, Oklahoma, and Texas. In Oklahoma, the USGS [US Geological Survey] recently acknowledged that wastewater disposal from fracking is a "contributing factor" to the sixfold increase in the number of earthquakes in that state. In addition, fracking has been found to contribute directly to seismic events, and even if the earthquakes that fracking directly generates are small, fracking could be contributing to increased stress in faults that leave those faults more susceptible to otherwise naturally triggered earthquakes of a greater magnitude.

Fracking Increases the Amount and Duration of Drilling

Fracking not only brings new risks but also increases the damage from oil and gas drilling because it allows the development of areas that were previously uneconomical to develop, and allows continued production from wells that might otherwise be retired. The scale of this threat should not be underestimated: California's Monterey shale, which extends offshore, holds an estimated 15.4 billion barrels of shale oil, or 64 percent of the nation's total shale oil resources, according to the U.S. Energy Information Administration. At a time when most of the Pacific Outer Continental Shelf is under a moratorium for new oil and gas leasing, fracking makes it

2. What impact do the authors foresee that a ban on drilling would have on consumer prices?

3. Why does a ban on offshore gas drilling have a greater impact on prices than the ban on offshore oil petroleum drilling, according to the authors?

Responding to the BP oil leak, President [Barack] Obama instituted a moratorium on deepwater (over 500 feet) drilling. Though a judge ruled against the moratorium, drilling has not restarted. In addition, though no official moratorium was issued for drilling in shallower water, the permitting process has slowed considerably.

The president has raised questions about the long-term necessity for drilling. Others would take this argument much further and ban all drilling offshore.

To help policy makers evaluate the arguments for limiting or eliminating offshore drilling, this [viewpoint] analyzes the economic impact of a total offshore drilling ban on the U.S. economy. The authors use a mainstream model of the U.S. economy to simulate a policy change that prevents new wells from being drilled and allows offshore production to decline as the current set of wells reach the end of their productive lives.

Nipping Expansion in the Bud

The Department of Energy's Energy Information Administration (EIA) projects that daily petroleum production will rise 18 percent between 2010 and 2035 and that daily production from offshore wells (in the lower 48 states) will rise by over 40 percent. EIA also predicts that offshore drilling will supply significant increases in natural gas production. While total natural gas production will rise 16 percent over the same period, offshore production of natural gas will rise 63 percent, at which time it will be nearly a fifth of total domestic production.

The reserves of petroleum are projected to rise by 5 billion barrels—even after extracting 57 billion barrels over the period 2010–2035. This happens because improvements in technology and price increases make previously uneconomic deposits economically viable. Further, because exploration and development are costly, it makes little sense to incur the costs of finding and extracting reserves that will not be used for decades.

In short, petroleum can be a major energy source for many decades. Consequently an offshore drilling ban's impact on the U.S. would be felt for decades.

For example, between now and 2035 an offshore drilling ban would:

- Reduce GDP [gross domestic product] by $5.5 trillion,

- Reduce the average consumption expenditures for a family of four by $2,381 per year (and exceeding $4,000 in 2035),

- Reduce job growth by more than 1 million jobs by 2015 and more than 1.5 million jobs by 2030, and

- Increase the total expenditures for imported oil by nearly $737 billion.

Effects on Consumer Prices

A permanent drilling ban would create a wedge between projected domestic oil production without the ban and the lower production levels with the ban in place. The lost petroleum output would have several impacts on the price of imported oil and thus consumer prices. For example, such a ban would necessitate the purchase of more imports to compensate for the lost domestic production. Because oil trades on world markets, this lost domestic production would cause world oil prices to rise—compounding the cost of the increased imports. The losses mount slowly, which means that the impact

Drilling in the Atlantic Would Benefit the Economy

Allowing access to the Atlantic OCS [Outer Continental Shelf] for oil and natural gas exploration and production activities would increase employment, economic activity, and government revenues over the long term with comparatively little additional spending required by federal and state governments. The nation as a whole, but especially the Atlantic coast states would likely see large employment increases, increased economic activity and increased government revenue as well as increased domestic oil and natural gas production, increasing the nation's energy security.

Quest Offshore Resources,
"The Economic Benefits of Increasing U.S. Access to Offshore Oil and Natural Gas Resources in the Atlantic," December 2013.

on oil prices and import costs will also mount slowly. The additional imported-oil cost exceeds $25 billion per year by 2018 and rises to over $45 billion per year by 2035.

Though, in percentage terms, the ban cuts domestic natural gas production half as much as domestic petroleum production, the price impact is greater because the natural gas market is predominantly regional, while the petroleum market is worldwide. Thus, there is less ability to buffer the domestic natural gas production cuts with additional imports. An offshore drilling ban, therefore, would likely lead to natural gas price increases of 10 percent by 2015, 23 percent by 2020, and 45 percent by 2035.

Since energy is a critical input for so many things, raising its cost will increase production costs throughout the economy. Though producers will pass most of the costs on to consumers, consumers will not be able to buy as much at these higher prices. Therefore, the higher energy prices cut the demand for all the other inputs, such as labor. As the higher costs for petroleum and natural gas ripple through the economy, there may be a few bright spots (such as suppliers of more energy-efficient capital goods), but the overall impact is decidedly negative.

An offshore drilling ban cuts domestic energy production, raises energy costs, and shrinks the nation's economic pie. The broadest measure of economic activity, gross domestic product (GDP), drops $5.5 trillion over the period 2011–2035. Employment levels fall below those projected to occur without a ban in place. By 2020, employment would be 1.4 million jobs lower than without the ban. By 2030, the projected gap reaches 1.5 million jobs.

Of course, shrinking the economy makes families poorer. By 2020 the annual reduction in disposable income for a family of four exceeds $2,000. This lost income exceeds $3,000 per year in 2030 and is over $4,000 per year in 2035.

Pulling the Rug Out

Petroleum and natural gas play a vital role in the U.S. economy and are likely to remain critical to economic activity for decades to come. The Department of Energy expects offshore production to be a bigger supplier of the nation's energy needs in the years ahead.

If a total ban on offshore drilling is implemented by 2011, then by 2035 Americans could expect national income (GDP) to drop by $5.5 trillion, total costs of imported oil to rise by $737 billion, total disposable income to decrease $54,000 per family of four, and job losses to exceed 1.5 million. A total ban on offshore drilling would pull the rug out from the economy's incipient recovery.

"Should we compromise our hundreds
of thousands of tourism and fishing jobs
for a mere few thousand drilling jobs?"

Drilling in the Atlantic Could Hurt the Economy by Damaging Tourism

Chris Carnevale

Chris Carnevale is coastal climate and energy coordinator at Southern Alliance for Clean Energy. In the following viewpoint, Carnevale argues that it would be detrimental to open the South Atlantic coastal waters to offshore gas and oil drilling. He states that noises from the air-gun testing used in offshore drilling would result in the deaths of thousands of marine mammals and would disrupt migratory and mating habits. Although drilling in the Atlantic would create jobs, these job opportunities would be far offset by the loss of jobs in tourism and fishing, Carnevale concludes.

As you read, consider the following questions:

1. How does the author counter the argument that off-shore drilling will bring down gas prices?

2. How many total jobs are at risk if the South Atlantic is opened to offshore drilling, according to the author?

3. How much total revenue is at risk if the South Atlantic is opened to offshore drilling, according to the author?

Today, April 20, marks the 4th anniversary of the tragic Deepwater Horizon Gulf [of Mexico] oil disaster. In spite of how apparent it seemed four years ago that offshore drilling is a bad idea whose time has gone, today we are facing the threat of *even more* drilling off our beautiful coasts. As we've reported before, the federal government is considering opening the Atlantic coast to offshore oil and gas exploration for the first time in 30 years. Yet the lessons learned from the Deepwater Horizon blowout have not been fully incorporated into industry practice or government regulation. On this four-year anniversary, we want to emphasize the reasons why it is a bad idea to drill off the Southeast Atlantic coast.

Oil and Gas Exploration Is Bad for Our Region

The current proposal by the federal government to open the Atlantic to offshore oil and gas exploration includes the use of seismic air-gun testing. This type of testing involves creating large blasts of noise that help show where petroleum deposits are. The noises are so loud, though, that they can damage hearing and navigation of marine mammals like whales and dolphins as well as other marine creatures. According to the federal government, allowing this testing would result in the death or injury of up to 138,500 marine mammals by 2020 and disrupt migratory and mating habits of many creatures including sea turtles. European studies have shown declines in catch rates for commercially important fish due to seismic air-gun testing. [Editor's note: In July 2014, the Bureau of Ocean Energy Management released a record of decision on the matter of Atlantic oil and gas exploration and did indeed open the Mid- and South Atlantic areas to seismic air-gun testing.]

Offshore Drilling Would Not Bring Economic Benefits

Exploration is just the beginning. The end goal is drilling. And the economics of drilling in the South Atlantic just don't make sense.

Contrary to what some politicians would have us believe, jeopardizing our coast with offshore drilling would not bring down gasoline prices. Studies under George W. Bush's administration have shown that if we opened all feasible offshore U.S. areas to drilling, the gas price MIGHT decline by no more than 3 cents per gallon by 2030. Since the U.S. supplies only 11 percent of the world's oil supply, we don't get to set the price. It's the international market that does that. As for natural gas, the U.S. is awash in cheap onshore gas due to recent technological improvements. Furthermore, more than 70 percent of the currently leased area for offshore drilling is sitting idle and unused. So why would we want to harm our marine and coastal environment exploring for oil and gas that the market doesn't call for, that won't decrease fuel prices, and for which there are plenty of other places to go?

As for local economic development due to oil and gas extraction, it likely won't be that great. Allow me to draw some examples from my home state of South Carolina to illustrate the point. Previous surveys have concluded that the geologic conditions for large deposits of oil and natural gas do not exist off our coast and as a result, it has been pointed out by the South Carolina Department of Commerce that "offshore natural gas drilling will likely not have a significant direct economic impact" and the South Carolina Board of Economic Advisors has said that "there does not seem to be much incentive to drilling off South Carolina at current prices."

Jobs and Revenue in Fisheries, Tourism, and Recreation at Risk from Seismic Air Guns and Offshore Drilling

State	Fisheries, Aquaculture & Seafood Markets GDP	Tourism & Recreation GDP	Tourism & Recreation Jobs	Recreational Fishing Jobs	Commercial Fishing Jobs
Delaware	$14,222,630	$492,990,932	13,408	1,270	407
Maryland	$116,071,142	$2,630,675,068	59,641	5,714	14,778
Virginia	$573,719,022	$1,962,257,873	85,514	5,167	19,064
North Carolina	$156,743,452	$982,666,376	30,380	17,221	8,479
South Carolina	$10,604,779	$2,401,134,933	55,485	5,035	1,169
Georgia	$69,138,081	$522,716,897	13,927	1,613	7,390
Florida	$284,717,845	$15,185,649,774	293,385	27,445	64,744

Source: Compiled by Oceana from NOAA National Marine Fisheries Service data.

TAKEN FROM: Chris Carnevale, "Why We Should Not Drill Offshore the South Atlantic," *CleanEnergy Footprints*, April 20, 2013.

To be sure, if the oil and gas industry were to develop in the Southeast, there would be some new jobs and economic development; but it must be recognized that these jobs would represent a direct threat to our bread-and-butter industries of tourism and fishing. We know from experience that offshore drilling and tourism can be at great odds. To drill offshore might jeopardize the estimated 80,000 coastal tourism jobs in South Carolina, which generate over $3.5 billion each year or the 350,000+ coastal tourism and fishing jobs in Florida that generate over $15 billion per year. As we saw with the BP Gulf oil disaster, oil spills decimate tourism and fishing industries. Should we compromise our hundreds of thousands of tourism and fishing jobs for a mere few thousand drilling jobs?

> "Natural gas is easier to deal with than oil, since it doesn't float on the surface and foul beaches or animals."

Why the Latest Gulf Leak Is No BP Disaster

Christopher Joyce

Christopher Joyce is a correspondent on the science desk of NPR. In the following viewpoint, he claims that the explosion in the Gulf of Mexico in July 2013 that caused a natural gas leak is very different and far less serious than the Deepwater Horizon oil rig blowup that leaked oil into the Gulf in 2010. In the 2013 incident, it appears that only gas, and not oil, leaked into the Gulf, he explains, and gas forms a liquid that quickly evaporates.

As you read, consider the following questions:

1. Why does oil spill expert and chemist Chris Reddy believe that the July 2013 explosion is unlikely to produce the devastating effects of the BP Deepwater Horizon oil spill?

2. Why do observers on the scene believe that leaking gas, and not oil, is probably occurring in the Gulf of Mexico following the July 2013 explosion?

3. According to the viewpoint, how does petroleum engineer Tadeusz Patzek say that gas ruptures are repaired?

Teams of workers are mobilizing in the Gulf of Mexico to try to stem a natural gas leak at an offshore drilling rig that exploded and caught fire Tuesday. The rig off the Louisiana coast has been partially destroyed by the out of control blaze, and firefighting boats are on the scene.

While that might call to mind images of the BP oil disaster in 2010, experts say the incidents are vastly different.

Chris Reddy, an oil spill expert and chemist from the Woods Hole Oceanographic Institute, was among the scientists who followed the fate of the BP spill, when the Deepwater Horizon oil rig blew up and leaked millions of gallons of oil into the Gulf.

Reddy says that while deep-sea gas reservoirs may sometimes contain oil, it's highly unlikely the accident at Well A-3 adjacent to a "Hercules 265 jack-up rig" would leak anything like the BP spill.

Observers reported seeing a thin sheen on the ocean surface Tuesday. But the latest reports from the federal Bureau of Safety and Environmental Enforcement say the sheen has since dissipated—unlike the vast stretches of sheen from the BP spill that fouled fragile marshlands along the Gulf coast.

The lack of sheen suggests the only thing crews have to deal with is leaking gas, according to Tadeusz Patzek, a petroleum engineer at the University of Texas, Austin.

A lot of reservoirs in the Gulf of Mexico are gas-rich or gas-only, Patzek explains. Many wells produce both gas and "hydrocarbon liquids" such as ethane, propane and butane. These liquids can form a sheen on the water's surface but are quick to evaporate.

That's especially true with hot weather and windy conditions, Reddy notes. "These thin light sheens they are seeing, they can go away relatively quickly," he says.

So far, bureau officials say they haven't determined how the gas leak started or where it is. With the platform still on fire, repair crews can't yet get close enough to investigate. A spokesperson for the agency says beams supporting some of the rig have collapsed.

The jack-up rig is owned by Hercules Offshore, which is based in Houston, and the well is owned by Walter Oil & Gas. The Bureau of Safety and Environmental Enforcement reports that the well platform and rig are located 55 miles offshore in 154 feet of water. Tuesday's blowout occurred while workers were constructing a "sidetrack well" to connect with an existing wellbore that extends down to the seafloor.

One way to stem the flow of natural gas is to drill a relief well—a standard emergency measure to stop uncontrolled flows from oil and gas wells.

BP drilled relief wells during the Deepwater Horizon spill. These are drilled into the seafloor and then toward the original well, which they intercept to divert the flow into new, secure wells. With BP's Macondo well, that process took months.

Patzek says if the gas rupture is at the platform, engineers won't have to drill relief wells into the seabed to divert the flow and extinguish the rig fire. Instead, they'll just need to deprive the flames of oxygen on the platform.

"Gas is gas," Patzek says. "You need to snuff it out by whatever means possible." That would be a combination of water and foam, the same sort of firefighting technique used for oil rigs that are on fire. Once they find the source of the leak, they can plug it or divert the flow through new pipes.

If the break is on the seafloor where the wellbore penetrates the earth, gas could be flowing into the ocean. But natural gas is mostly made up of methane, and in deep wells, the methane would most likely dissolve before it gets to the surface.

Once dissolved, it's eaten by bacteria. "Methane is the best thing they can eat," Patzek says.

In the Deepwater Horizon accident, lots of natural gas as well as oil escaped into the water before the Macondo well was capped. Scientists determined that methane-eating microbes degraded much of that gas without evidence of serious harm to the environment.

And, of course, natural gas is easier to deal with than oil, since it doesn't float on the surface and foul beaches or animals.

"This is no Macondo oil spill," Patzek says.

> *"This ... shows how taking oil and gas production to technical extremes carries significant risks."*

Total Leak Underlines Offshore Gas Risks

James Herron, Alexis Flynn, and Sarah Kent

James Herron, Alexis Flynn, and Sarah Kent are reporters for the Wall Street Journal. In the following viewpoint, the authors argue that a gas leak from Total S.A.'s Elgin platform in the North Sea in March 2012 demonstrates that the risk of gas leaks is higher in more challenging drilling environments. The Elgin field presents "an unprecedented technical challenge" because of reservoir pressures four times higher than the North Sea average, the reporters explain.

As you read, consider the following questions:

1. What types of incidents are likely to be the most frequently encountered in challenging drilling environments, according to the authors?

2. According to a report written by seven Total employees in 2009, what are some signs that the Elgin and Franklin reservoirs are becoming more unstable?

3. According to Jean-Louis Bergerot, what are some reasons why it is more challenging to drill in high-pressure, high-temperature environments?

The five-day battle to stem a dangerous gas leak from Total S.A.'s Elgin platform in the North Sea highlights the increased risks of exploiting high-pressure and high-temperature oil and gas reservoirs, which are seen as an increasingly important part of the U.K.'s dwindling resource base.

These types of fields are thought to contain a significant proportion of the U.K.'s remaining oil and gas, making them important enough to have been targeted with a specific tax break to encourage development. Yet documents show that the French oil-and-gas producer's Elgin and Franklin fields off the coast of Scotland—at the extreme end of the spectrum of high-pressure and high-temperature fields—have faced major technical challenges, from their discovery right up until the incident that triggered the gas leak.

Paris-based Total has played down the risks of an explosion, but in the wake of BP PLC's deepwater Gulf of Mexico oil spill two years ago this latest incident shows how taking oil and gas production to technical extremes carries significant risks. The European Union Thursday said it may need to amend a proposal for stricter safety rules on offshore drilling as a result of the leak, as technical reports emerged that highlight how well-control incidents are likely to be the most frequently encountered in challenging drilling environments.

Total says the gas is leaking from a point some 4,000 meters (13,200 feet) below the seabed into a wellbore that had previously been shut down. Total workers first detected problems four weeks ago but were forced to evacuate the Elgin platform Sunday after they lost control of pressure in the well and flammable gas and condensate spewed into the facility.

The gas cloud that resulted at the Elgin platform is potentially explosive, and industry experts say it could destroy the platform if it ignites. Total insists the risk of an explosion is low, because the weight of the condensate and the prevailing wind will stop it from making contact with the still-burning flare on the platform.

Documents viewed by Dow Jones Newswires show that the risk of this type of incident—an unexpected leakage of gas into a previously stable wellbore, resulting in loss of control—is far greater in high-pressure, high-temperature fields like Elgin. The reports, authored by engineers from Total and the rest of the industry, show how the company has struggled to manage this risk for almost a decade, although up until this week it had apparently done so successfully.

A spokesman for the U.K. Health and Safety Executive, which oversees workplace-safety issues, said a report it commissioned in 2005 produced a set of guidelines for drilling wells on high-pressure, high-temperature fields, and it checks regularly for compliance with them.

"HSE is revisiting the issues with operators of other [high-pressure, high-temperature well] developments," said HSE spokesman Jason Green.

The EU may amend a proposal for stricter safety rules on offshore drilling, once it has more information about the causes of the natural-gas leak at the Elgin field, said Marlene Holzner, spokeswoman for energy issues.

Shortly after Elgin and Franklin went into production, a Total presentation described development of these fields as an "unprecedented technical challenge" because of reservoir pressures four times higher than the North Sea average. On its website, the company outlines how it had to create new technology and techniques to tap the fields.

Total has a 46% stake in the Elgin and Franklin fields. Other partners include Italy's Eni E +1.17% SpA with 22%; the U.K.'s BG Group BG.LN +0.05% PLC with 14%; German utility E.ON AG EOAN.XE +2.01%'s Ruhrgas subsidiary with

5%; and U.S. companies ExxonMobil Corp. XOM +1.52% and Chevron Corp. CVX +0.71%, each with 4%.

A later report prepared by engineering consultants Highgoose Ltd. in 2005 for the U.K. Health and Safety Executive warned that despite industry successes in overcoming these technical challenges, "there remains a general concern that not all high pressure/high temperature hazards have been identified yet."

The report warned that well-control incidents, like the one immediately prior to the current leak, are likely to be the most frequently occurring problem on these types of fields.

In 2009, a report written by seven Total employees and submitted to the U.K. Geological Society, noted that as the Elgin and Franklin reservoirs became depleted, they became even more unstable.

Three earthquakes occurred on the Elgin boundary fault in 2007 and 2008, and there were signs that geological stresses resulting from huge pressure changes were deforming the rocks around the reservoir, the report said.

This meant "the threat of a well failure could become reality," it said.

In October 2011, a report from Jean-Louis Bergerot, a manager in Total's drilling division, acknowledged that managing high-pressure, high-temperature reservoirs was still very challenging and paradoxically getting more difficult as time passes.

"In fields such as Elgin/Franklin, wells are exposed to multiple threats resulting from the large amount of depletion," Mr. Bergerot wrote in a paper for the Society of Petroleum Engineers. As gas is pumped out of the reservoir, its pressure drops relative to the surrounding rock, unleashing powerful stresses.

The steel casing that lines a well can be buckled or deformed by movements in the rock, Mr. Bergerot said. "Eventually, the liner may become sheared off completely," he said.

Arctic Drilling Should Be Stopped

Ten days after the leak began, Total [S.A.] is still struggling to contain the gas pouring from its North Sea Elgin platform . . .

In the past 30 years, we've lost 75 per cent of the Arctic sea ice. Drilling for and burning more fossil fuels in its melting waters is pretty much the last thing we should be doing.

It's reckless. It's stupid. It's plain wrong.

"Lessons from the Elgin Gas Leak: Why We Must Stop Shell's Arctic Drilling," Greenpeace.org, April 4, 2012.

Most well liners on the Elgin and Franklin fields have been affected in some way by this process, Mr. Bergerot said.

Total has said that in the current incident, gas is probably entering the well through a leak in its casing.

Faults in the rock can also reactivate with little warning and allow oil and gas to move to unexpected places within the rock formation, Mr. Bergerot said. This means that wells "may face high levels of gas in the formation where the initial development wells did not encounter any hydrocarbon," he said.

Total has said the source of the current gas leak is likely to be gas found in a layer of rock above the main reservoir on the Elgin field.

Mr. Bergerot also notes the difficulty of controlling pressure in wells that cross layers of rock subject to extreme pressure differences. Oil companies use large quantities of mud to prevent oil and gas from surging up boreholes. In wells with very high pressure differences, however, the amount of mud must be very finely controlled and the risk of a kick that could send gas surging up through the borehole to blow out at the surface is high, he said.

It was a surge of gas and condensate from the well onto the Elgin platform that forced the evacuation Sunday.

David Hainsworth, health, safety and environment manager at Total U.K., said the company has been actively managing these issues for a long time. "What we've been doing over the past two or three years is plugging and abandoning those old wells," which have had their casings compromised, he said.

The well that is now leaking was shut down 12 months ago on the suspicion that it had failed, "but we hadn't got round to the final plugging and abandonment exercise; we'd just been monitoring the well," Mr. Hainsworth said. There is nothing to suggest this job was done inadequately prior to the leak, he said.

Analysts said that tighter scrutiny of operators of high-pressure, high-temperature fields is likely. "We expect the [Elgin] field to be shut down for the rest of 2012 even if the leak is swiftly resolved, due to likely stringent inspections of the other wells," said analysts from Jefferies in a note to clients. "There may also be knock-on implications for operators of similar high-pressure fields, such as Statoil, Conoco and Shell."

Tighter restrictions on these fields could have wider implications for U.K. energy supply. The Department of Energy and Climate Change estimated in 2009 that between 12% and 15% of the total number of U.K. offshore oil and gas discoveries and prospects are of the high-pressure, high-temperature variety.

Industry body Oil and Gas U.K. estimates that between 14 billion and 24 billion barrels of oil equivalent in oil and gas remain untapped in U.K. waters. Even recovering the low end of this estimate will require substantial advances in the exploitation of high-pressure, high-temperature, and other types of more complex fields, it said in its 2011 economic report.

Periodical and Internet Sources Bibliography

The following articles have been selected to supplement the diverse views presented in this chapter.

Ann Chapman	"N.C. Needs Offshore Oil and Gas Activity," *StarNewsOnline*, January 6, 2014.
Dan Chu	"No New Oil Drilling in Our Oceans," *Huffington Post*, August 29, 2014.
Economist	"Gas in the Eastern Mediterranean: Drill, or Quarrel?," January 12, 2013.
Daniel J. Graeber	"Gulf Rig Fire: How Safe Is Offshore Natural Gas Drilling?," *Christian Science Monitor*, July 25, 2013.
Michael T. Klare	"Rushing for the Arctic's Riches," *New York Times*, December 7, 2013.
Ryan Koronowski	"Critic of Offshore Drilling Safety Regulation Helps Run Company That Owns Failed Natural Gas Rig," *ClimateProgress*, July 25, 2013.
Lacey McCormick	"Another Rig Fire in the Gulf, Another Wakeup Call," *Wildlife Promise*, July 24, 2013.
John Murawski	"Opening Atlantic Ocean to Offshore Drilling Likely," *News and Observer*, October 2, 2012.
Stanley Reed	"Cracking the Energy Puzzles of the 21st Century," *New York Times*, October 14, 2013.
Paula C. Squires	"New Study Says Virginia Among Top Three States to Benefit from Offshore Gas and Oil Drilling," *Virginia Business*, December 5, 2013.
Loren Steffy	"Don't Drive to the Coast and Complain About Offshore Drilling," *Forbes*, August 31, 2014.

For Further Discussion

Chapter 1

1. Rock Zierman contends that fracking is a safe technology that poses no environmental threats, while Anthony Ingraffea argues that fracking releases toxins into the air and water. Considering each argument, with which author do you agree, and why?

2. Both Anthony Ingraffea and Louis W. Allstadt urge the development of alternative energy sources. What are some of these sources, and what are some of the benefits and problems with these sources?

Chapter 2

1. Marcus Stern and Sebastian Jones write about pipeline safety being challenged by too few regulations and inspectors, while Karl Henkel reports that pipeline safety is improving. Are you concerned about gas pipeline safety? What steps could be taken to improve safety? Explain.

2. Lena Groeger compares gas pipeline safety to airline safety—transporting gas by pipeline is safer than by truck or rail, and airplanes are safer than cars. However, on the rare occasion when something goes wrong, the results can be devastating. She goes on to say that this analogy can only be carried so far; that there are some significant differences between pipelines and airlines. Are there aspects of airline safety that you think should be applied to pipelines? What are these, and why could they be helpful?

Chapter 3

1. Michael Levi concludes that the benefits of exporting natural gas outweigh the negatives, while Craig Segall claims fracking poses environmental risks. Based on the

evidence each author uses to support his position, what is your view on exporting natural gas? Explain your reasoning.

2. Josiah Neeley suggests that exporting natural gas to America's European allies could strengthen these countries. How would you weigh the potential political benefits of exporting gas against some of the downsides? Offer evidence to support your reasoning.

Chapter 4

1. Emily Jeffers argues that offshore fracking harms air, water, wildlife, and health, with damages that are severe and often irreversible. If you were a member of the California Coastal Commission, the organization to which Jeffers directs her argument, would you be compelled to vote to halt fracking for oil and gas off the California coast? Explain your reasoning.

2. David W. Kreutzer and John L. Ligon support offshore drilling for gas on the basis that it will create jobs. On the other hand, Chris Carnevale argues that the jobs lost by offshore drilling will be greater than the jobs gained. What types of jobs are most likely to be gained by offshore drilling, and what types of jobs lost? What action on offshore drilling do you recommend, and why?

Organizations to Contact

The editors have compiled the following list of organizations concerned with the issues debated in this book. The descriptions are derived from materials provided by the organizations. All have publications or information available for interested readers. The list was compiled on the date of publication of the present volume; the information provided here may change. Be aware that many organizations take several weeks or longer to respond to inquiries, so allow as much time as possible.

American Gas Association (AGA)
400 North Capitol Street NW, Washington, DC   20001
(202) 824-7000
website: www.aga.org

The American Gas Association (AGA) represents local energy companies distributing natural gas to their customers. It advocates on behalf of its members in both federal and state regulatory arenas. It publishes fact sheets, *American Gas Magazine*, and a variety of other publications, including "2013 Gas Facts: A Statistical Record of the Gas Industry."

Center for Biological Diversity
PO Box 710, Tucson, AZ   85702-0710
(520) 623-5252 • fax: (520) 623-9797
e-mail: center@biologicaldiversity.org
website: www.biologicaldiversity.org

The Center for Biological Diversity is a nonprofit organization whose purpose is to protect endangered species through legal action and activism. It publishes newsletters and research reports, including "Endangered Earth, Summer 2013."

Center for Climate and Energy Solutions
2101 Wilson Boulevard, Suite 550, Arlington, VA   22201
(703) 516-4146 • fax: (703) 516-9551
website: www.c2es.org

The Center for Climate and Energy Solutions is a nonprofit, nonpartisan independent organization dedicated to educating the public and key policy makers about the causes and potential consequences of global climate change. By releasing reports on environmental impacts, policy issues, and economics, the center works to encourage the domestic and international communities to reduce emissions of greenhouse gases. It was formed in November 2011 as the successor to the Pew Center on Global Climate Change.

Clean Energy Group (CEG)
50 State Street, Suite 1, Montpelier, VT   05602
(802) 223-2554 • fax: (802) 223-4967
website: www.cleanegroup.org

The Clean Energy Group (CEG) is a nonprofit advocacy organization working in the United States and internationally on technology, finance, and policy programs in the areas of clean energy and climate change. Among CEG's publications is "Getting Gas Right: A Regional Climate Strategy."

Council on Foreign Relations (CFR)
The Harold Pratt House, 58 East Sixty-Eighth Street
New York, NY   10065
(212) 434-9400 • fax: (212) 434-9800
website: www.cfr.org

The Council on Foreign Relations (CFR) is an independent, nonpartisan think tank and publisher whose mission is to help provide clarity to the foreign policy choices facing the United States. The CFR website offers testimonies, op-eds, reports, and articles such as "The Good News About Gas," as well as archives of its flagship magazine *Foreign Affairs*.

Global Warming International Center
22W381 Seventy-Fifth Street, Naperville, IL   60565-9245
(630) 910-1551 • fax: (630) 910-1561
website: www2.msstate.edu/~krreddy/glowar/glowar.html

The Global Warming International Center is an international organization that disseminates information concerning global warming science and policy. It serves both governmental and nongovernmental organizations as well as industries in more than one hundred countries. The center sponsors research on global warming and its mitigation. It publishes the quarterly journal *World Resource Review*.

International Energy Agency (IEA)
9, rue de la Fédération 75739, Paris   Cedex 15
  France
(33) 1-40-57-65-00 • fax: (33) 1-40-57-65-09
website: www.iea.org

The International Energy Agency (IEA) is an autonomous organization that works to ensure reliable, affordable, and clean energy for its twenty-eight member countries and beyond. The IEA's four main areas of focus are energy security, economic development, environmental awareness, and engagement worldwide. Among its publications are "World Energy Outlook 2013" and "Key World Energy Statistics 2013."

Natural Gas Supply Association (NGSA)
1620 Eye Street NW, Suite 700, Washington, DC   20006
(202) 326-9300
website: www.ngsa.org

The Natural Gas Supply Association (NGSA) represents major integrated and large independent domestic producers of natural gas. NGSA actively pursues opportunities to promote natural gas as a reliable and environmentally friendly source of energy. It publishes fact sheets, analyses, and studies on the benefits of natural gas, including the series Manufacturing Renaissance.

Sierra Club
85 Second Street, Second Floor, San Francisco, CA   94105
(415) 977-5500 • fax: (415) 977-5797

e-mail: information@sierraclub.org
website: www.sierraclub.org

The Sierra Club is a member-supported public interest organization that promotes conservation of the natural environment by influencing public policy decisions in the legislative, administrative, legal, and electoral arenas. It publishes books; the monthly *Sierra Magazine*; and a newsletter, *The Planet*, which comes out ten times a year.

United States Energy Association (USEA)
1300 Pennsylvania Avenue NW, Suite 550, Mailbox 142
Washington, DC   20004-3022
(202) 312-1230 • fax: (202) 682-1682
website: www.usea.org

The United States Energy Association (USEA) is an organization of public and private energy-related organizations, corporations, and government agencies. The USEA represents the interests of the US energy sector by increasing awareness of energy issues. The USEA prepares a variety of publications on the energy market.

United States Environmental Protection Agency (EPA)
1200 Pennsylvania Avenue NW, Washington, DC   20460
(202) 272-0167
website: www.epa.gov

The Environmental Protection Agency (EPA) is the agency of the US government that coordinates actions designed to protect the environment. It conducts assessments, research, and educational activities to maintain and enforce environmental standards. Among its reports is "Study of the Potential Impacts of Hydraulic Fracking on Drinking Water Resources."

Bibliography of Books

Walter M. Brasch   *Fracking Pennsylvania: Flirting with Disaster*. Carmichael, CA: Greeley & Stone, Publishers, 2013.

Canadian Association of Energy and Pipeline Landowner Associations (CAEPLA)   *A Revolution Underground: The History, Economics & Environmental Impacts of Hydraulic Fracturing*. Calgary, AB: CAEPLA, 2012.

Russell Gold   *The Boom: How Fracking Ignited the American Energy Revolution and Changed the World*. New York: Simon & Schuster, 2014.

John Graves   *Fracking: America's Alternative Energy Revolution*. Ventura, CA: Safe Harbor International Publishing, 2012.

Richard Heinberg   *Snake Oil: How Fracking's False Promise of Plenty Imperils Our Future*. Santa Rosa, CA: Post Carbon Institute, 2013.

Peter Hoffmann   *Tomorrow's Energy: Hydrogen, Fuel Cells, and the Prospects for a Cleaner Planet*. Cambridge, MA: MIT Press, 2012.

Robert W. Kolb   *The Natural Gas Revolution: At the Pivot of the World's Energy Future*. Upper Saddle River, NJ: Pearson, 2013.

Ezra Levant   *Groundswell: The Case for Fracking.*
                       Toronto: McClelland & Stewart, 2014.

Michael Levi   *The Power Surge: Energy, Opportunity,*
                       and the Battle for America's Future.
                       New York: Oxford University Press,
                       2013.

Abrahm   *Hydrofracked?: One Man's Mystery*
Lustgarten   *Leads to a Backlash Against Natural*
                       Gas Drilling. New York: ProPublica,
                       2011.

Seamus McGraw   *The End of Country: Dispatches from*
                       the FrackZone. New York: Random
                       House, 2011.

Tara Meixsell   *Collateral Damage: A Chronicle of*
                       Lives Devastated by Gas and Oil
                       Development and the Valiant
                       Grassroots Fight to Effect Political and
                       Legislative Change. Seattle, WA:
                       CreateSpace, 2010.

Edmund C.   *Environmental Accounting for Oil and*
Merem   *Natural Gas: A North American Case*
                       Study of Canada and the Southeast of
                       the United States. Lewiston, NY:
                       Edwin Mellen Press, 2010.

Bill Powers   *Cold, Hungry and in the Dark:*
                       Exploding the Natural Gas Supply
                       Myth. Gabriola Island, Canada: New
                       Society Publishers, 2013.

Alex Prud'homme   *The Ripple Effect: The Fate of Fresh*
                       Water in the Twenty-First Century.
                       New York: Scribner, 2011.

Peter Ralph	*Dirty Fracking Business.* Melbourne, Australia: Melbourne Books, 2012.
Vikram Rao	*Shale Gas: The Promise and the Peril.* Research Triangle Park, NC: Research Triangle Institute, 2012.
Suzana Sawyer and Edmund Terence Gomez, eds.	*The Politics of Resource Extraction: Indigenous Peoples, Multinational Corporations and the State.* New York: Palgrave Macmillan, 2012.
Bob Shively and John Ferrare	*Understanding Today's Natural Gas Business.* Laporte, CO: Enerdynamics, 2009.
US Department of Energy	*Modern Shale Gas Development in the United States: A Primer.* Los Gatos, CA: Progressive Management, 2011.
David A. Waples	*The Natural Gas Industry in Appalachia: A History from the First Discovery to the Tapping of the Marcellus Shale.* Jefferson, NC: McFarland, 2012.
Tom Wilber	*Under the Surface: Fracking, Fortunes, and the Fate of the Marcellus Shale.* Ithaca, NY: Cornell University Press, 2012.
Gregory Zuckerman	*The Frackers: The Outrageous Inside Story of the New Billionaire Wildcatters.* New York: Penguin, 2013.

Index

A

Accountability issues, pipeline damage, 82, 89, 91–92, 95
Activism
    anti-fracking, 47, 50–51
    Ukraine politics, 170
    See also Environmental groups
Air pollution
    fracking contributions, 36, 39–40, 134, 135–136, 144, 199, 202, 204–205
    fracking does not cause, 30, 32, 34–35
    natural gas vs. coal, 22–24
    oil seeps, 193, 196
    regulations, 32
    See also Carbon dioxide emissions
Air travel, 111–112
Air-gun testing, 216, 217–218, 219*t*
Alaska
    development potential, 156–157
    reserves, 148
Allen, Bruce, 190–198
Allen, David, 54
Allentown, Pennsylvania, 69, 93, 94, 113
Allstadt, Louis W., 41–51
American Council for Capital Formation, 172
American Petroleum Institute, 100–101, 105
American Public Gas Association, 15

Anadarko Petroleum Corporation, 58, 64
Ancient Greece, 15
Anti-subsidy duties, 182–184
Apache Corporation, 58, 64
Arctic region
    drilling and leaks, 229
    reserves, 44, 148, 225
Arkansas
    oil spills, 101, 107–108
    seismic events, 209
Asia
    gas imports, 126–127, 151, 152, 156
    natural gas prices, 125, 126
    offshore drilling claims, 188–189
    See also specific countries
Assad, Mary-Leah, 80–81
Associated Industries of Massachusetts, 77, 81
Association of Oil Pipe Lines, 115–116
Atlantic coast economy, 216, 219*t*, 220
Atlantic Ocean drilling, 214, 216–220, 225–230
Australia, gas production and exporting, 151, 156, 157
Azerbaijan, 192

B

Baltimore, Maryland, 15
Bamberger, Michelle, 207
Bandow, Doug, 143

C

United States, 2010–2035, 22, 23*t*

See also Methane emissions

Carnevale, Chris, 216–220

Cattle, 207

Center for Biological Diversity, 199, 200

Ceres (environmental investment group), 56, 57, 58, 59, 61, 62–65

"Changing the Game?: Emissions and Market Implications of New Natural Gas Supplies" (report, Stanford University), 20, 21–24

Chemical industry. *See* Petrochemical industry

Chemical wastes, fracking, 201–204

Cheniere Energy, 127

Chesapeake Energy, 58, 64–65

Chevron, 53, 228

Chhatre, Ravindra, 103–104

China

gas demand, 153

history of oil and natural gas, 14–15, 192

offshore drilling claims, 188–189

trade potential, 131, 182–183, 184

Chu, Steven, 160

Clean Air Act (1963), 202

Climate change

adaptation, 50

coal regulations, 53–54

fracking contributions, 21, 22, 41–51, 136, 137, 144, 206

fracking does not contribute, 20, 21, 22, 52–55

gas pipeline leak contributions, 83, 86

moving past fossil fuels, including natural gas, 79

natural gas exports contribute, 136, 145

President Obama address on, 43, 50

Coal

gas production and use, 15

global warming regulations, 53–54

natural gas compared, 20, 21, 22, 50, 53–54, 83–84

natural gas switches, 59, 72, 77

Colorado

fracking and emissions, 39, 205

seismic events, 209

wells drilled, 59, 64

Columbia Gas Ohio, 91, 94, 95–96

Common Ground Alliance, 107

Companies. *See* Petroleum industry; Utility companies

Components, natural gas, 14

Congress

House of Representatives Natural Resources Committee, 82–92

opposition to gas exports, 159–168

regulatory challenges and blocks, 104–106, 108, 158

Senate energy policy research and reporting, 83

support of gas exports, 146–158, 184–185

underfunds pipeline regulation and safety, 99, 101–102

Congressional Research Service, 116, 117, 149, 178

Conoco, 230

volume potential, 209, 212–213

Ohio
improving pipeline safety, 93–98
pipeline accidents, 94, 95–97, 98
seismic events, 209
shale gas, 72, 78

Oil and Gas UK, 230

Oil industry. *See* Petroleum industry

Oil seepage, natural, 190, 191–196, 197

Oil spills
causes, 113–114
correction and cleanup attempts, 117
Deepwater Horizon oil disaster (2010), 37, 217, 220, 221, 222, 223–224
fracking-related, 203
offshore oil production, 194
pipelines, United States, 97–98, 101, 107–108, 110, 117

Oklahoma
gas fields, 16
seismic events, 209

Organisation for Economic Co-operation and Development (OECD) countries, 153

Oswald, Robert E., 207

Otsego, New York, 42, 47, 48

P

Pacific Gas and Electric, 104–105

Patrick, Deval, 84

Patzek, Tadeusz, 222, 223–224

Pawlowski, Ed, 69

PEMEX, 196–197

Pennsylvania
fracking and water recycling, 59–60
history, oil excavation, 192
pipeline explosions, 69, 87, 93, 94, 113
pipeline leaks policy and reporting, 89, 91–92, 92

Pennsylvania Utility Commission, 69, 89, 91–92

Perry, Mark, 175

Petrochemical industry
gas as raw material, 21, 140, 175
gas exports effects and opinions, 130–131, 133, 141, 142, 143, 155, 165–166

Petroleum industry
alternative energy development, 49
fracking, 53
gas market reports, 151
natural gas export attitudes, 133
offshore drilling investment, 227–228, 230
responsibility, and lack thereof, for pipeline upkeep, 82, 83–85, 88, 94–95, 100–101, 104–105, 116–117
water buying/recycling, for fracking, 58, 59, 65–66

Philippines, offshore drilling claims, 188

PHMSA. *See* Pipeline and Hazardous Materials Safety Administration (PHMSA)

Physical properties and qualities, natural gas, 14

Pipeline and Hazardous Materials Safety Administration (PHMSA)